Contents

Introduction

In the early 1960s, the Nature Conservancy formed a section at the Monks Wood Experimental Station to investigate the effects of pesticides on wildlife. At that time, much concern over certain uses of organochlorine insecticides had arisen, following the mass deaths of birds and other wildlife on farmland. Preliminary surveys revealed high concentrations of organochlorines in birds of prey and some freshwater bird species. Several such species were thought to have declined in numbers as a result of this contamination. In 1964, a research programme was begun under I. Prestt on some of these species. The programme had two main themes. First, there were post-mortem examinations and analyses of pesticide residues in birds found dead and submitted by members of the public. Second, there were studies on field populations, both by national surveys and by detailed investigation of the year-to-year trends in numbers and breeding success in particular localities. The programme was later extended to include polychlorinated biphenyls (PCBs) and mercury.

In 1973, the Research Branch of the Nature Conservancy became part of the Institute of Terrestrial Ecology (ITE), and this work was continued in ITE by A.A. Bell and R.K. Murton, much of it supported by a contract from the Nature Conservancy Council (NCC). One of the main reasons for continuing the monitoring programme was to check on the effectiveness of restrictions that have been imposed on some uses of the chemicals. The scheme is unique in providing residue data on British wildlife over a 15-year period, and it is still continuing.

This book gives the residue levels found in bird tissues and eggs during the period 1963-1977, and discusses the findings. The main contaminants investigated were DDE (from DDT), HEOD (from dieldrin and aldrin), PCBs and mercury.

The chemicals and their uses

DDT *(1,1,1-trichloro-2,2-di(chlorophenyl)ethane)*

Like other organochlorine insecticides, DDT does not occur naturally. It was first synthesised in the 1870s, but its insecticidal properties were not appreciated until the Second World War. Soon after the War, DDT was used widely in Britain in horticulture and agriculture, as well as in homes and gardens, and by industry and health authorities. In vertebrate tissues, the fat-soluble metabolite of DDT most commonly found is DDE. Many organisms, especially those in the higher trophic levels of a food web, are exposed via their food to DDE rather than to DDT. In this report, only DDE figures are quoted. Amounts of other DDT-type compounds found in the samples were relatively low.

The Advisory Committee on Poisonous Substances used in Agriculture and Food Storage (Advisory Committee) considered in 1964 that "no restrictions should be placed on the current uses of DDT in agriculture, horticulture, home gardens and food storage practice, but its use should be reviewed at the end of three years" (Cook 1964). When the Advisory Committee next reported, it recommended that various uses of DDT in agriculture, horticulture, food storage, dry cleaning and domestic situations should cease "as soon as can be arranged" (Wilson 1969). The Ministry of Agriculture, Fisheries and Food (MAFF) issues each year a *List of Approved Products and their Uses for Farmers and Growers.* In the Foreword to the issue for 1971, the following statement was made with regard to the 1969 recommendation: "The Government accepted this recommendation and with the agreement of the manufacturers has taken steps to withdraw the recommendations for the uses in question by 30th September, 1971." Despite these restrictions, DDT is still used on agricultural and horticultural crops to control a variety of invertebrate pests, as shown in the *List of Approved Products and their Uses for Farmers and Growers, 1980.* (Further restrictions were brought into force

HEOD *(dieldrin)*

The cyclodiene group of organochlorine insecticides was used on a widespread scale in Britain from the mid-1950s. Like DDT, cyclodienes had many different uses against insect pests. The cyclodiene residue that is found most frequently in wildlife samples is 1,2,3,4,10,10-hexachloro-6,7-epoxy-1,4,4a,5,6,7,8,8a-octahydro-1,4-endo,exo-5,8-dimethanonaphthalene (HEOD) which is the active ingredient of the commercial insecticide dieldrin. Dieldrin contains 85% HEOD. In addition, HEOD is formed in the environment as a metabolite of the active ingredient of another widely used cyclodiene, aldrin.

Aldrin and dieldrin were especially effective against wireworms, carrot fly and wheat bulb fly and gave protection against fly strike in sheep. These chemicals were also believed to have been responsible for numerous incidents in the late 1950s, involving the deaths of countless birds and mammals. When used as a seed dressing on wheat to control the bulb fly, these toxic and persistent compounds were ingested by grain-feeding birds, which were then taken by predators or scavengers. In the summer of 1961, government, industry and farming representatives agreed to a voluntary ban on cyclodiene insecticides on grain planted in the spring, as birds were most vulnerable at that time of year (for a detailed account, see Mellanby 1967). Later the Advisory Committee recommended that seed dressings containing these compounds should be used only on "winter sown wheat (up to the end of December) where there is a real danger of attack from wheat bulb fly" (Cook 1964). In practice, drilling was often delayed because of bad weather, and spring sowing of dressed wheat continued to cause some problems for many years (eg see Prestt, Jefferies & Macdonald 1968). The Advisory Committee also proposed that "the use of aldrin and dieldrin dips and sprays for sheep should be discontinued". This ban came into operation in 1966. Further restrictions were recommended by the Advisory Committee in 1969 (Wilson 1969). As with DDT, certain uses of dieldrin had disappeared by 1972 from the *List of Approved Products and their Uses for Farmers and Growers*. It was not until December 1975, however, that dieldrin was finally withdrawn as a seed dressing. Although organochlorines in agriculture have largely been replaced by organophosphate and carbamate insecticides, dieldrin continues to be used intensively in moth-proofing and wood preservation.

PCBs

Polychlorinated biphenyls (PCBs) are industrial pollutants and are not deliberately released into the environment, as are pesticides. Like DDT and HEOD, they are organochlorine compounds which persist for long periods. They have been manufactured since the 1930s for use in hydraulic fluids, transformers, paints, inks, adhesives, etc., and have somehow seeped into the environment (for a general account, see Moriarty 1975). During the manufacturing process, chlorine is passed through biphenyl to produce mixtures of compounds chlorinated to varying degrees. These various chlorinated biphenyls differ widely in their chemical and physical properties, but only total PCB residues are given in this book (see p.12).

The extent of contamination of the environment with PCBs was not suspected until the late 1960s. With the advent of the electron-capture detector, analysts of environmental material had been aware of 'interfering' compounds for several years, but it was only in 1966 that these compounds were identified as PCBs. The discovery that PCBs were common and widespread (eg see Prestt, Jefferies & Moore 1970) evoked a prompt reaction from Monsanto Chemicals, the sole manufacturers of PCBs in Britain and the United States. Monsanto withdrew PCBs from all uses from which they were most likely to contaminate the environment, this ban becoming effective in Britain early in 1971.

It is also worth noting that PCBs can be formed when DDT vapour is irradiated with ultraviolet light, but the extent of this transformation in the natural environment is not known.

Mercury

Mercury differs from the organochlorines because it occurs naturally in many forms, both free and bound, with variations in properties and toxicity. As is often the case with metals, it can be difficult to define how much of that found is 'natural' and how much is 'pollutant' (Bull *et al.* 1977; Osborn 1978). Man's activities, however, have resulted in elevated mercury levels in several parts of the world, with concern over its effects on people and wildlife.

Sweden has experienced considerable problems from mercury contamination (see Berg *et al.* 1966; Moriarty 1975). There, the most important sources were from phenylmercury acetate used as a fungicide in the wood pulp industry and from mercury used in the electrolytic manufacture of chlorine and caustic soda in chlor-alkali plants. Methylmercury is regarded as being the most toxic form, at least to man, and can be produced in the freshwater environment from mercury in other forms. In addition, organo-mercury compounds have long been used as agricultural fungicides, though the alkylmercury types were banned in Sweden from 1966.

In Britain, only about 5% of the mercury used is in agriculture; by far the largest tonnage is used in the chlor-alkali industry (HMSO 1976). The agricultural fungicides used here are generally based on the safer aryl form of mercury (Sly 1972).

Residues in bird tissues

Materials and methods

From 1963, dead birds (Plate 1) have been sent to Monks Wood in response to advertisements in popular ornithological journals and conservation magazines. Most of the specimens were in fairly good condition when received (Plate 2). They were stored at −20°C until autopsy, when body weight and condition were recorded (Plate 3), and an effort was made to establish the likely cause of death. As a consequence of this examination, together with details supplied by the finder, birds were allocated to one of the following categories describing the likely reason for death.

(1) Trauma. Such birds were believed to have died as a consequence of a specific trauma resulting from hitting a motor vehicle, flying into wires, shot wounds, etc.

(2) Poor-condition. These were specimens with signs of infection and/or poor body condition. Birds that might have lost weight from starvation, or which were in very poor body condition for any other reason, were

Plate 1.   Collection of dead birds of prey sent in by the public for organochlorine analysis at Monks Wood.
Photo: I. Wyllie.

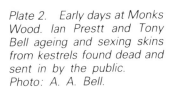

Plate 2.   Early days at Monks Wood. Ian Prestt and Tony Bell ageing and sexing skins from kestrels found dead and sent in by the public.
Photo: A. A. Bell.

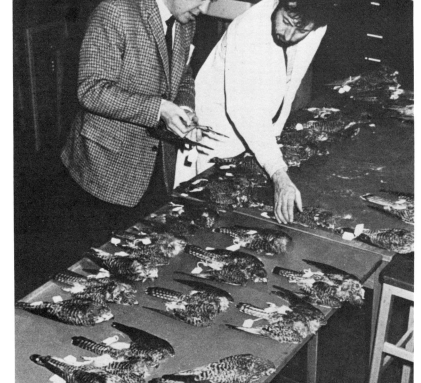

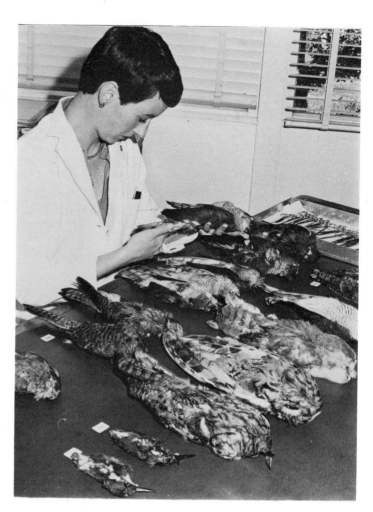

Plate 3. Examining birds used in the monitoring programme for body condition before dissection. Photo: I. Wyllie.

Plate 4. Using the gas-liquid chromatograph for organochlorine residue analysis of birds of prey liver samples.
Photo: I. Wyllie.

allocated to this category, as they resembled birds suffering from diseases, such as avian tuberculosis, but without having obvious symptoms. Such specimens proved to be the least useful in studies of environmental pollutants.

(3) Remainder. These were specimens that could not be assigned to either of the previous categories. Many such birds were found to show signs of haemorrhage, especially in the brain. Subsequently, this condition was found to be often associated with high residues of HEOD in the liver. A separate 'haemorrhage' category was not distinguished in this report, because, unlike the other categories, the detection of haemorrhages was found to depend to an appreciable extent on the skill and experience of the investigator. For other birds in this category, there was no obvious cause of death.

These categories are in priority order and are exclusive, so that a road casualty also found to be diseased is placed in the trauma category.

Samples from various tissues were removed for analysis of pollutant residues, but most attention was focussed on the liver. This organ is comparatively large, is easily removed and contains pollutants at relatively high concentration. Recently, it was found that the liver undergoes seasonal cycles in weight, protein and fat content (Osborn 1979), and that the general physical condition of the bird affects the proportion of the total pollutant load carried in the liver (Bogan & Newton 1977). These last authors, amongst others, have advocated analysis of brain tissue as the indication of organochlorine poisoning in birds (but see also Jefferies & Davis 1968). Such problems were not appreciated when this work began, and for continuity the liver has remained the standard organ for analysis.

Most tissue samples were analysed for organochlorine residues by gas-liquid chromatography in the Laboratory of the Government Chemist; levels were expressed as parts per million (ppm) wet weight. DDE and HEOD were identified down to 0.1 ppm, PCBs to 1.0 ppm, and amounts less than these given as '$<x$', trace or nil detected. For DDE and HEOD, 0.001 is the value assigned to nil detected, 0.005 for trace (0.01 and 0.05 for PCBs); values '$<x$' are taken as '$0.5x$'. DDE and HEOD analyses date back to 1963, and PCBs to 1967. The mercury determinations were all made in 1975 and 1976 on samples that had been stored for up to seven years, and should therefore be treated with some caution. Mercury in tissues is known to be rather volatile, and the older carcases had been unfrozen previously for autopsy and for the removal of tissue samples for organochlorine analysis. Total mercury content in each sample was determined at Monks Wood by digestion in nitric acid followed by flameless atomic absorption spectrophotometry (Hatch & Ott 1968). Residues were expressed as ppm dry weight.

Initially, a wide range of species was collected and analysed, but it became apparent after a few years that some carried only low residues, so these were dropped from the scheme to save cost. Ten species were collected and analysed throughout, namely grey heron (Ardea cinerea), sparrowhawk (Accipiter nisus), kestrel (Falco tinnunculus), barn owl (Tyto alba), great crested grebe (Podiceps cristatus), kingfisher (Alcedo atthis), golden eagle (Aquila chrysaetos), rough-legged buzzard (Buteo lagopus), peregrine (Falco peregrinus) and long-eared owl (Asio otus). For the first four species, samples have been analysed from more than 100 individuals.

Objectives

(1) To establish pollutant levels in dead birds of different species, and, if possible, to determine the significance of these residues.

(2) To determine, in those species for which there were sufficient samples, how residue levels varied from month to month, from year to year, and from region to region within Britain. The results on annual changes helped to indicate how effective the various restrictions imposed on organochlorine use had been.

(3) To identify aspects that merit further investigation.

Organochlorine residues in samples of herons, sparrowhawks, kestrels and barn owls

To understand the significance of the pollutant levels found, it will help first to give some details of the status and ecology of the main species in Britain.

i. **Grey heron** (Plate 5): This heron breeds throughout Britain, and each year since 1928 the British Trust for Ornithology (BTO) has organised a national census of nests (Nicholson 1929). The usual population in England and Wales is about 4500 pairs, but a severe winter may reduce these numbers by as much as 50%, with up to three years normally required for recovery (Reynolds 1974; Sharrock 1976).

Most herons in Britain nest colonially in trees, and feed primarily on fish. At a colony in Lincolnshire, adults were found to feed mainly on eels (Anguilla anguilla), roach (Rutilus rutilus) and bream (Abramis brama) from nearby rivers and dykes (Prestt 1970). They also take a variety of other food items, such as amphibians and water voles (Arvicola terrestris) (British Ornithologists' Union (BOU) 1971).

The tissues and eggs of herons proved to be highly contaminated with organochlorine residues; egg shell thinning (a response to DDE/DDT, widespread amongst predatory birds — see Ratcliffe 1970; Cooke 1973a) was marked, and shell breakage prevalent in colonies which were studied (Prestt 1970; Cooke et al. 1976) (Plate 6). On the origin of the residues, Prestt commented: "DDT and dieldrin have not been applied on any large scale directly to rivers and drainage channels, so in the main these chemicals must have entered the aquatic systems accidentally as industrial and agricultural effluents or as fall-out from the atmosphere.... The residues present in the fish in the herons' feeding grounds, during the heron breeding season, all contained similar relatively low levels. This suggests that some herons may normally carry a high residue load through feeding regularly on fish which contain relatively low residues."

Outside the breeding season, our herons disperse widely within Britain. In addition, continental immigrants reach all parts of Britain, mainly during the period August to April.

ii. Sparrowhawk (Plate 9): The sparrowhawk is the commonest small raptor of wooded areas. Populations showed a marked decline during the period 1956-63, largely as a consequence of lethal poisoning by cyclodienes, but for some years previously they had experienced reduced breeding success associated with egg shell thinning (Prestt 1965; Ratcliffe 1967, 1970; Prestt & Ratcliffe 1972; Newton 1974). Following restrictions on cyclodiene use, populations soon began to recover, and are now almost back to strength in western and northern districts, where there is little arable cultivation (eg Newton 1973). However, they are still scarce in the most intensively cultivated parts of eastern England. The British population is resident throughout the year, but some north European birds winter here, while others pass through on migration (Newton 1975).

Sparrowhawks nest in woods, and hunt in both woods and open country. They live almost entirely on other birds (Newton & Blewitt 1973; Brown 1976). Females weigh about twice as much as males and capture bigger prey, so that the sexes differ in their food spectrum: females regularly kill birds as large as woodpigeons *(Columba palumbus)*, which were the most frequent victims of seed-dressings in the 1960s (eg see Cramp *et al.* 1962), and female sparrowhawks might, therefore, be expected to have been more at risk than males to lethal doses of cyclodienes via this route. It has often been proposed that larger predatory birds have acquired lethal HEOD residues by consuming just a few highly-poisoned pigeons (see discussion in Jefferies & Prestt 1966). Both sexes would have taken passerines that had fed on dressed grain, or had acquired DDT, or other organochlorines from invertebrates in orchards or arable fields (Davis 1968; Jefferies & Davis 1968; Moreton & Kite 1975).

iii. Kestrel (Plate 11): This bird is probably the most numerous and familiar raptor in Britain, breeding in a wide variety of habitats, including city centres. Populations declined in eastern England in the late 1950s and early 1960s, again probably as a result of cyclodiene poisoning, but changed little over the rest of the country (Prestt 1965; Prestt & Bell 1966; Prestt & Ratcliffe 1972). Kestrels remain sparse in the East

Anglian Fens, but this may be due in part to lack of suitable nest sites and feeding areas (Sharrock 1976).

The British breeding population is partly migratory, with some birds staying near their breeding areas all year, and others moving south for the winter, reaching as far as France and Spain (Mead 1973).

Normally kestrels hover when looking for prey, most often the short-tailed vole *(Microtus agrestis)* (Brown 1976). The bank vole *(Clethrionomys glareolus)* and the wood mouse *(Apodemus sylvaticus)* are other important prey (Jefferies *et al.* 1973; Brown 1976). Small mammals feeding on arable fields can accumulate pesticide residues from seed dressings and represent one route by which kestrels may acquire organochlorines and mercury (Jefferies *et al.* 1973; Jefferies & French 1976). Kestrels also hunt from perches and take birds and invertebrates, as well as mammals (Yalden & Warburton 1979).

iv. Barn owl (Plates 13, 18): Barn owls are widespread in Britain as far north as central Scotland (Sharrock 1976). There is evidence of a slow, long-term decline in numbers, at least since the 1930's and of a marked decrease in eastern England during the late 1950s and early 1960s, again coinciding with the widespread use of cyclodienes in agriculture (Prestt 1965).

The barn owl is mainly sedentary in Britain. Birds of the northern European race, *Tyto alba guttata,* occur here occasionally from August to April.

When hunting, barn owls fly slowly along hedges and verges and over rough ground. The short-tailed vole and wood mouse are commonly taken, and contaminated specimens of the latter species in particular may have resulted in many barn owls acquiring residues of HEOD and mercury from dressed grain (Jefferies *et al.* 1973). These owls have habitat and food preferences which overlap appreciably with those of kestrels, and the numbers of both species fluctuate in parallel in normal conditions, following the cycles of their rodent prey (Snow 1968; Murton 1971).

Statistical treatment

Given that one of the main objectives of the scheme was to monitor the effect on residue levels of restrictions in chemical usage, the programme suffered from some unavoidable deficiencies. First, the species studied were of conservation value and could not be collected, and sacrificed for chemical analysis. Second, residues in birds found dead might have differed from those in live birds, and the resulting data had to be interpreted with this in mind. In particular, residues can be mobilised from the fat depots of a starving or dying bird so that the levels in the liver and other tissues increase (see Jefferies & Davis 1968; Robinson & Crabtree 1969; Ecobichon & Saschenbrecker 1969; Parslow & Jefferies 1977; Bogan & Newton 1979). Third, the data were further complicated by seasonal, annual and regional variations in residue levels, and other differences due to sex and age. So, not surprisingly, the complete batch of samples for any one species was extremely heterogeneous.

Differences between species were expected, as no two species are exactly alike in ecology or physiology, although the kestrel and barn owl are similar in some respects.

So which sectors of a population were represented by carcases in the various categories of death? Imagine a simplified hypothetical population (Table 1), containing birds in either of two states of health (healthy and poor) and two levels of contamination (low and high), so that four types of birds exist at one time: (1) healthy low, (2) poor low, (3) healthy high, and (4) poor high. The trauma category of carcases would probably contain birds of all four types, though not necessarily in the same proportions as the living population, since a bird with high residues might be more or less liable to get hit by a car than one with low residues. The poor-condition category would by definition contain only birds of health types 2 and 4. The remainder category would contain birds of health type 3 that had died from organochlorine poisoning, together with birds from all four health types that had died from miscellaneous other causes.

HEOD appear to die during a short period of the year and may die relatively quickly close to where they acquired their residues, they are unlikely to die as a result of a trauma. On the other hand, sublethal residues may alter their behaviour and make them more likely to become road casualties. In support of this hypothesis, impaired vision was suspected in pigeons contaminated by endrin, another cyclodiene insecticide (Revzin 1966). Probably the trauma group tends to be more representative of the living population with respect to residue levels than does the entire sample, especially if immediate pre-death or post-mortem redistribution of residues occurs to a great extent in diseased, starved or poisoned birds. The approach adopted here is to examine data both for the trauma group separately and for all samples together.

The tendency for the fat-soluble pollutant residues to be mobilised together could have resulted in misleading conclusions. For instance, HEOD may have caused death, but with an associated mobilisation and concentration of DDE in the liver, so that DDE residues may have been artificially high in this organ in months when deaths due to HEOD were prevalent.

Toxic residues in wildlife samples tend not to be normally distributed in the statistical sense. This fact has been appreciated by a number of authors (eg Robinson 1967; Robinson et al. 1967), who have used

TABLE 1

A simplified avian population presented as an aid to deciding the likely composition of the groups of samples assigned to the different categories of death — see text.

'Health type'	Relative number of individuals	General health	Tissue residue levels	Relative proportion dying	Reasons for death
1	Many	Healthy	Low	Low	Trauma, miscellaneous
2	Some	Poor	Low	Intermediate	Trauma, disease, miscellaneous
3	Some	Healthy	High	Intermediate	Trauma, poisoning, miscellaneous
4	Very few	Poor	High	High	Trauma, disease, poisoning, miscellaneous

There are conflicting views about which death categories best reflect the situation in the living population. Stanley and Elliott (1976) used owls that were traffic victims, and implied that analysis of all birds found dead led to bias because of the inclusion of poisoned birds and of specimens that had starved and concentrated their residues in the organs being analysed. Mellanby (1967) observed that "analyses of road casualties seem to agree fairly well with those of birds which have been shot, so they probably give a fairly accurate picture". Bell and Murton (1977) held a different view, based on analysis of kestrel carcases held at Monks Wood: "samples collected from roadsides under-represent the incidence of deaths resulting from dieldrin poisoning". Since birds poisoned by

geometric means. In this report, geometric means with the range of values within 1 geometric standard error on either side are used unless stated otherwise.

In addition to calculating geometric means, the data were examined to find the proportion of samples with residues in the following ranges: 0-0.9 ppm, 1.0-9.9 ppm, 10-99 ppm, and 100 ppm or more. Results expressed in this way were most useful in assessing temporal and geographical variations. The significance of liver residues of 1, or 10, or 100 ppm can be difficult to define. A question of particular interest was what residue levels were indicative of death. For HEOD, some authors have suggested that residues greater than 10 ppm wet weight indicate that the bird died from HEOD poisoning (Moore 1965; Prestt *et al.* 1968; Prestt & Jefferies 1969), while other authors have suggested levels of up to 20 ppm (Robinson 1969; Bunyan *et al.* 1975). Generally, there is agreement that the critical level is of the order of 10 ppm. The study of Jefferies and Davis (1968) on HEOD poisoning in song thrushes *(Turdus philomelos)* showed that birds accumulated HEOD in the liver up to a level of a few ppm, but, above a certain limit, the liver lost weight and HEOD concentration increased rapidly and death followed. Thus, "a bird with a concentration of 3 ppm of dieldrin in the liver or brain may be much closer to the lethal concentration than was previously suspected". There appears to be little information on the effects of lower levels of HEOD in the liver, although laboratory pigeons with less than 3 ppm HEOD in the liver have shown behavioural and hormonal aberrations (S. Dobson pers. comm.).

DDE levels need to be at least 100 ppm wet weight in the liver to imply poisoning by DDT-type compounds (see Jefferies 1967; Robinson 1969; Porter & Wiemeyer 1972; Bunyan *et al.* 1975). Few carcases examined here had liver residues of more than 100 ppm DDE, but, in those that did, the levels often far exceeded 100 ppm. In the absence of other information, the deaths of such birds were attributed to DDE poisoning. Of more interest is the level at which there may have been sublethal effects. Liver residues of 10 ppm DDE have been associated with hyperthyroidism, change in heart weight and function, and alterations in the production of adrenal corticosterone (Jefferies & French 1971; Srebocan *et al.* 1971). DDE has also been observed to exert behavioural and hormonal effects in caged pigeons at liver levels of less than 4 ppm (S. Dobson pers. comm.). A liver residue of at least 10 ppm DDE is taken to mean that the bird could have suffered sublethal effects.

What has been said about DDE also applies to PCB residues, but with the additional complication that PCBs are mixtures of compounds with different chemical and toxicological properties. The convention remains simply to sum the individual peaks on the chromatograph trace and quote total residues. It seems that liver residues must be greater than 100 ppm to indicate death by poisoning (see Prestt *et al.* 1970; Parslow *et al.* 1973). Few of the liver samples examined here contained 100 ppm or more PCBs. Sublethal effects have been noted at lower levels. Guillemots *(Uria aalge)* treated with Aroclor 1254, a commercial PCB mixture, had increased thyroid weights, associated with a liver concentration of 20 ppm PCBs (Jefferies & Parslow 1976). Japanese quail *(Coturnix coturnix japonica)* dosed with Aroclor 1260 showed increased formation of δ-aminolevulinic acid associated with a liver residue of only 1.4 ppm (Vos *et al.* 1971). Many of our samples had residues of 10 or more ppm; such levels may have been sufficient to cause sublethal effects.

Preliminary examination and presentation of the data

In general, data were analysed for the years 1963-1975, because, during this period, there was a continuous sequence of material. Some of the kestrel data for 1975 were incomplete and, whenever necessary, calculations for this species were done on material collected up to 1974. In 1976, only carcases collected during the first few months of the year were analysed.

i. **Comparison of residue levels in the livers and brains of kestrels:** To find whether a relationship existed between liver and brain residues, tissues from 15 kestrels were analysed, 11 from birds in the trauma group and 4 in the remainder group (Figure 1 shows DDE residues as an example). For the trauma group, residues in liver were positively related to those in brain for each organochlorine. Spearman Rank Correlation coefficients were: HEOD, $R=0.90$ ($P<0.01$); DDE, $R=0.83$ ($P<0.01$); PCBs, $R=0.75$ ($P<0.01$). Remainder birds fitted the same general pattern. Providing the bird has not starved, the residue level in the liver would seem to be an equally useful indicator of overall content as the level in the brain (see also Bogan & Newton 1977).

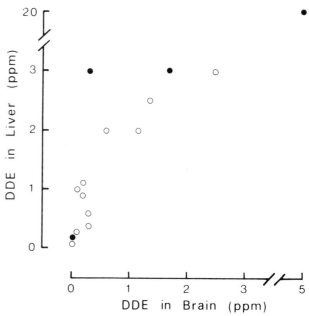

Figure 1. *Kestrel: relationship between DDE in the liver and brain of 15 birds.* ○, *trauma;* ●, *remainder.*

ii. **Residues and category of death:** For kestrels, most of the birds in the trauma and poor-condition groups had liver residues of less than 5 ppm HEOD, whereas many of those in the remainder group had higher levels with a second peak at 15-20 HEOD (Figure 2). This observation is consistent with the remainder group containing many birds that had died for miscellaneous reasons with only low liver residues, together with other birds that had died from HEOD poisoning, with liver residues of 10 ppm or more. This second peak was not observed for the other organochlorines in the remainder group, or in liver samples from other species.

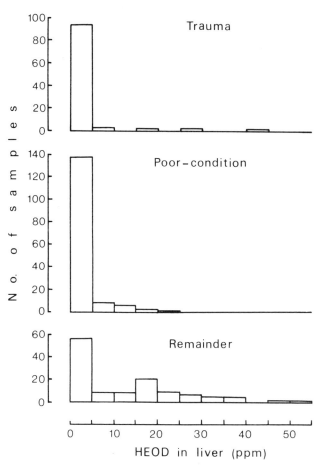

Figure 2. *Kestrel: numbers of livers showing different HEOD residues, according to category of death.*

iii. HEOD residues in livers of kestrels and sparrowhawks with signs of haemorrhage: Kestrels with signs of haemorrhage tended to have higher HEOD levels than sparrowhawks with similar symptoms (Figure 3). The histogram for the kestrel shows a broad band centred at about 20 ppm comprising birds whose livers contained at least 10 ppm HEOD: these birds had probably been poisoned lethally by HEOD. In 13 (30%) liver samples, however, HEOD levels were less than 5 ppm: it is unlikely that HEOD killed these birds (Prestt *et al.* 1968), and there is no reason to suspect that such levels induce haemorrhages, but this point requires clarification. The histogram for the sparrowhawk was different, lacking the broad band above 10 ppm. Perhaps very few of the sparrowhawks examined were poisoned by HEOD; only 7 out of 43 (16%) of this group contained 10 or more ppm HEOD in the liver. An alternative explanation is that the sparrowhawk is more susceptible to HEOD than the kestrel, dying with haemorrhage symptoms at lower levels of HEOD in the liver (see discussion in Prestt & Ratcliffe 1972). While this is only a tentative explanation, there is some supporting evidence. The declines noticed in the late 1950s and early 1960s, and which were blamed on cyclodienes, were much more severe in sparrowhawks than kestrels (Prestt 1965). More than 20% of the sparrowhawks examined were found to have haemorrhages which were not the result of a trauma. If many of these haemorrhages were not caused by HEOD, then another agent must have induced them on a widespread scale: perhaps DDE contributed here. The subject requires further study.

The remainder group of all species contained significantly more birds with high liver residues than did the trauma group, except for PCBs in kestrels (Table 2). For barn owls, there were also more birds with high residues in the poor-condition group (Table 2). Hence, the remainder groups of all species tended to contain the birds with the most contaminated livers.

iv. Residues in trauma groups: variations due to age and sex: There were two main reasons for determining whether variations in residue levels within the trauma groups were due to age and sex. First, it was of intrinsic interest to know whether sex and age differences occurred. Second, the trauma groups were used to study temporal and spatial variations, and any

TABLE 2

Numbers of birds with different residue levels grouped according to category of death, 1963-1975.

	Category of death	HEOD (ppm)				DDE (ppm)					PCBs (ppm)				
		0–0.9	1–9.9	≥10	Total	0–0.9	1–9.9	10–99	≥100	Total	0–0.9	1–9.9	10–99	≥100	Total
Heron	Trauma	44	13	3	60	21	23	14	2	60	13	25	11	3	52
	Poor-condition	6	8		14	1	5	7		13	1	5	6		12
	Remainder	22	30	17	69***	8	22	33	6	69***	4	12	33	2	51***
Sparrowhawk	Trauma	67	25	1	93	19	53	19	2	92	18	45	12		75
	Poor-condition	6	5		11	2	4	5		11	3	2	2		7
	Remainder	47	32	12	91**	16	34	35	6	91**	14	32	25		71*
Kestrel	Trauma	66	30	5	101	51	38	12		101	30	34	8		72
	Poor-condition	94	51	9	154	60	73	19	2	154	29	64	16	1	101
	Remainder	27	37	55	119***	30	61	24	4	119***	30	48	12		90
Barn owl	Trauma	85	34	4	123	86	35	2		123	64	31	2		97
	Poor-condition	9	22	4	35***	14	18	3		35**	11	10	4		25*
	Remainder	28	37	28	93***	33	35	22	3	93***	25	28	12		65***

χ^2 test: greater number of samples with high residues than in the trauma group of that species, *, $P<0.05$; **, $P<0.01$; ***, $P<0.001$.

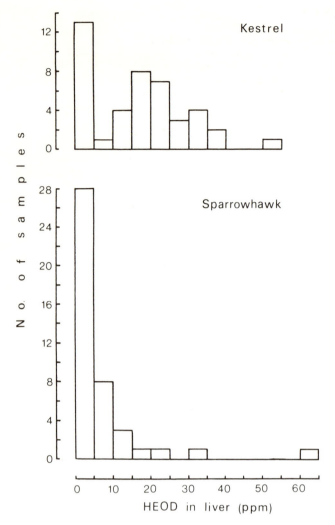

Figure 3. *Kestrel, sparrowhawk: numbers of livers showing different HEOD levels, from carcases with haemorrhage symptoms.*

unsuspected differences in residue levels between sex or age groups could easily prove misleading.

The barn owl is a more difficult bird to age than are the other species and was therefore left out of this investigation. Among herons, sparrowhawks and kestrels (Table 3), the only significant intra-species differences were between the age groups of sparrowhawks, the adults tending to contain more DDE and PCBs than the juveniles (birds up to a year old). This finding in sparrowhawks is of interest as Newton and Bogan (1978) reported that "clutches laid by yearling females on average contained significantly less of all OCs [organochlorines] than did those laid by older females". In herons and kestrels, too, adults tended to contain slightly more DDE and PCBs than juveniles, but not significantly so. In no species was there any significant difference between residues in males and females; the only combination that approached significance was HEOD in sparrowhawks, the females tending to contain higher residues ($0.1 > P > 0.05$). For none of the residues did all three species show a consistent tendency for one sex to have higher residues.

v. Residues in the remainder group of sparrowhawks: variations due to age and sex: Because the trauma group for sparrowhawks had suggested age and sex differences in residues, the remainder group for this species was examined as well. Residues were, in general, highest in this group, and it was hoped that a study of these samples would throw more light on the age and sex differences.

Adult sparrowhawks had significantly higher mean levels of all three organochlorine residues in the liver than did juveniles ($P < 0.001$). This result is again consistent with the study on egg residues made by Newton and Bogan (1978), in which adults laid more contaminated eggs than one-year-olds. Of equal importance, however, females had significantly higher mean residues of HEOD than males ($P < 0.01$). In fact, all the nine birds (of known age and sex) with HEOD residues of at least 10 ppm were females. Among sparrowhawks, only the females are sufficiently large and powerful to kill adult woodpigeons, so that males avoid acquiring lethal HEOD residues by this route. Males and females contained similar amounts of DDE, presumably accumulated from the passerines on which both sexes prey. Thus, the female sparrowhawk, because of its ability to take bigger prey, appears to have been at greater risk from HEOD poisoning. This risk will have been exacerbated by the female's habit of hunting more frequently over farmland (Newton 1979), where pigeons dying from HEOD poisoning were frequently available.

vi. Body weight and HEOD residues in the liver: Birds killed by organochlorines often have low body weight, little or no fat, and elevated levels of pollutants in the liver (eg see Jefferies & Davis 1968; Stickel *et al.* 1969; Porter & Wiemeyer 1972). A bird that has suffered a lingering death following a trauma may also have starved and mobilised residues from its fat depots. For this reason, statistical tests were carried out to determine whether, within the trauma groups, liver residue levels varied with body weight. A process that could also have raised the residue concentrations after death is tissue desiccation, as organochlorine levels are quoted as ppm wet weight.

In kestrels and herons, the birds with the lowest body weights had residues similar to birds of higher body weight (Figure 4 for kestrels), but, in sparrowhawks and barn owls, there was some tendency for birds with the lowest body weights to have higher-than-average residues. Generally, trauma birds of unspecified weight contained similar HEOD levels in their livers to birds of average weight, and, in statistical analyses in the following sections, all samples for the trauma groups were used irrespective of whether their body weights were known.

In all species, birds in the poor-condition category tended to be of lower weight than those in the trauma category, with birds in the remainder group intermedi-

TABLE 3

Trauma groups: residues in adults, juveniles, males and females, 1963-1975.

		No. of samples with residues (ppm)					Geometric mean (ppm) (range of values within 1 standard error)
		0–0.9	1–9.9	10–99	≥100	Total	
HEOD							
Heron	Adults	14	3	2		19	0.19 (0.09–0.38)
	Juvs	27	7	1		35	0.25 (0.17–0.37)
	Males	18	6	2		26	0.35 (0.23–0.55)
	Females	23	4	1		28	0.15 (0.09–0.25)
Sparrowhawk	Adults	32	8			40	0.42 (0.33–0.53)
	Juvs	28	17	1		46	0.33 (0.23–0.46)
	Males	32	8			40	0.25 (0.18–0.34)
	Females	28	17	1		46	0.52 (0.39–0.69)
Kestrel	Adults	18	9			27	0.62 (0.51–0.76)
	Juvs	26	14	5		47	0.70 (0.53–0.92)
	Males	26	12	1		39	0.63 (0.53–0.74)
	Females	20	11	4		35	0.72 (0.51–1.02)
DDE							
Heron	Adults	8	5	4	2	19	2.64 (1.59–4.39)
	Juvs	12	17	6		35	1.64 (1.29–2.07)
	Males	9	10	5	2	26	2.29 (1.57–3.35)
	Females	11	12	5		28	1.66 (1.24–2.21)
Sparrowhawk	Adults	3	25	11	1	40	4.60 (3.70–5.71)
	Juvs	13	24	7	2	46	2.51* (1.92–3.28)
	Males	7	27	6		40	2.77 (2.24–3.41)
	Females	9	22	12	3	46	3.90 (2.96–5.15)
Kestrel	Adults	11	13	3		27	1.10 (0.78–1.55)
	Juvs	27	14	6		47	0.99 (0.79–1.25)
	Males	19	15	5		39	1.06 (0.80–1.39)
	Females	19	12	4		35	1.00 (0.78–1.30)
PCBs							
Heron	Adults	4	6	1	2	13	2.39 (1.14–4.99)
	Juvs	10	17	6	1	34	1.99 (1.40–2.83)
	Males	9	10	5	1	25	1.47 (0.90–2.42)
	Females	5	13	2	1	22	3.13 (2.09–4.67)
Sparrowhawk	Adults	4	25	5		34	2.87 (2.37–3.48)
	Juvs	11	17	7		35	1.21[a] (0.84–1.76)
	Males	6	20	5		31	2.06 (1.54–2.75)
	Females	9	22	7		38	1.70 (1.24–2.35)
Kestrel	Adults	9	9	3		21	0.92 (0.56–1.52)
	Juvs	19	19	3		41	0.39 (0.26–0.58)
	Males	14	12	3		29	0.56 (0.35–0.91)
	Females	14	16	3		33	0.49 (0.32–0.75)

*χ^2 test: significantly different from adults, $P<0.05$
[a] t-test: significantly different from adults, $P<0.05$

ate (shown for kestrels in Figure 5). Birds with high HEOD residues in the remainder group tended not to have low body weight. If 10 ppm HEOD is taken to indicate death by poisoning, then the birds that succumbed in this manner were not underweight, but tended to be of average weight. Therefore, birds removed from the population by HEOD poisoning were not thin, sickly individuals, but were otherwise fit birds, probably capable of breeding.

When all carcases were considered together, those with at least 10 ppm HEOD in the liver were rarely encountered towards the ends of the spectrum of body weights. This fact is illustrated for the kestrel in Figure 6; in the weight range 160-180 g, 41% of the carcases had high HEOD residues in the liver (n=108), but levels of 10 ppm HEOD were never encountered in birds weighing less than 120 g or more than 220 g (n=42). The lack of high HEOD residues in heavy birds is likely to be due to the HEOD inducing a loss of body condition, ie any bird with at least 10 ppm HEOD in the liver has probably suffered from fat mobilisation and weight loss. One reason for the lack of high residues in birds of low weight was probably because many of these birds were juveniles which starved in autumn/winter, before they had much opportunity to accumulate high levels of HEOD (see p.18-21).

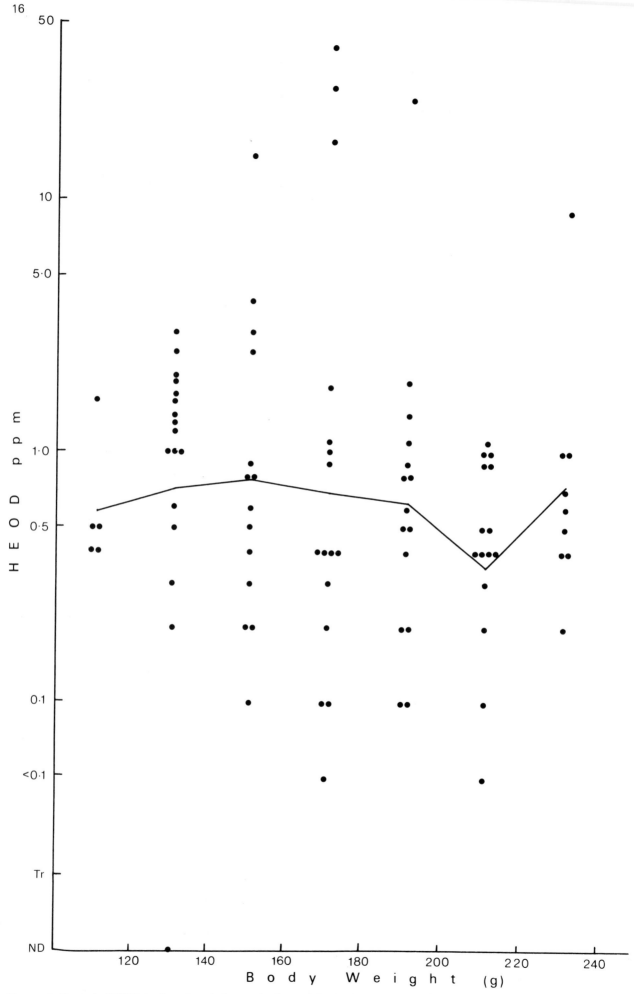

Figure 4. Kestrel: HEOD in liver in relation to body weight in the trauma group. ————, geometric means.

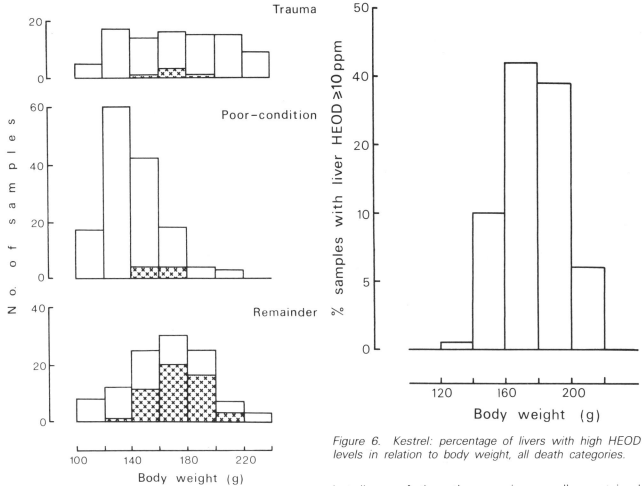

Figure 5. *Kestrel: body weights of birds in different death categories. Shaded areas show samples with at least 10 ppm HEOD.*

Figure 6. *Kestrel: percentage of livers with high HEOD levels in relation to body weight, all death categories.*

vii. Species differences in residues: Residue levels in the trauma group and in the total sample of each species are summarised in Table 4. The kestrel was taken as the reference species, as more samples were analysed for this than for the other species. Sparrowhawk livers contained less HEOD than kestrel livers,

but livers of the other species usually contained roughly similar concentrations to kestrels. For both DDE and PCBs, heron and sparrowhawk livers had higher residues than kestrels, while barn owl livers had lower residues.

The ratios of the three residues were similar for herons and sparrowhawks (Table 5), livers containing much more DDE and PCBs than HEOD. For kestrels and barn owls, however, DDE and PCBs were present in similar

TABLE 4

Residues in trauma groups and total samples, 1963-1975.

	Trauma group						Total samples					
	No. of samples with residues (ppm)					Geometric mean (ppm) (range of values within 1 standard error)	No. of samples with residues (ppm)					Geometric mean (ppm) (range of values within 1 standard error)
	0–0.9	1–9.9	10–99 (%≥10)	≥100 (%≥100)	Total		0–0.9	1–9.9	10–99 (%≥10)	≥100 (%≥100)	Total	
HEOD												
Heron	44	13	3(5)		60	0.27[a] (0.19–0.37)	72	51	20(14)		143	0.87 (0.71–1.07)
Sparrowhawk	67	25	1(1)		93	0.31[aa] (0.25–0.39)	120	62	13(7)		195***	0.50[aaa] (0.42–0.58)
Kestrel	66	30	5(5)		101	0.62 (0.53–0.72)	187	118	69(18)		374	1.20 (1.09–1.32)
Barn owl	85	34	4(3)		123	0.56 (0.49–0.65)	122	93	36(14)		251	1.21 (1.06–1.37)
DDE												
Heron	21	23	14(27)	2(3)	60*	2.36[aa] (1.86–2.98)	30	50	54(44)	8(6)	142***	5.29[aaa](4.51–6.20)
Sparrowhawk	19	53	19(23)	2(2)	93***	3.07[aaa] (2.59–3.64)	37	91	59(34)	8(4)	195***	4.42[aaa](3.88–5.04)
Kestrel	51	38	12(12)		101	1.03 (0.88–1.20)	141	172	55(16)	6(2)	374	1.59 (1.43–1.76)
Barn owl	86	35	2(2)		123***	0.35[aaa] (0.27–0.40)	133	88	27(12)	3(1)	251***	0.70[aaa](0.60–0.81)
PCBs												
Heron	13	25	11(27)	3(6)	52*	2.58[aaa](1.90–3.49)	18	42	50(48)	5(4)	115***	5.55[aaa](4.47–6.87)
Sparrowhawk	18	45	12(16)		75	1.60[a] (1.27–2.01)	35	79	39(25)		153**	2.02[aa] (1.69–2.41)
Kestrel	30	34	8(11)		72	0.60 (0.45–0.81)	89	146	36(13)	1(<1)	272	1.01 (0.87–1.17)
Barn owl	64	31	2(2)		97**	0.11[aaa](0.08–0.14)	100	69	18(10)		187***	0.24[aaa](0.20–0.29)

χ^2 test: significantly different from kestrel, *, $P<0.05$; **, $P<0.01$; ***, $P<0.001$.
t-test: significantly different from kestrel, [a], $P<0.05$; [aa], $P<0.01$; [aaa], $P<0.001$.

or lower concentrations to HEOD, and these two species might have been expected to resemble one another in their liver residues, since they have similar food habits. They were much more likely than herons or sparrowhawks to acquire HEOD residues directly from small rodents that had fed on dressed grain in the field, a fact that was reflected in their relatively higher HEOD residues.

TABLE 5

Ratios of geometric mean residues of HEOD, DDE, PCBs in liver samples, 1963-1975.

| | HEOD : DDE : PCBs | |
	Trauma group	Total samples
Heron	1 : 8.7 : 9.6	1 : 6.1 : 6.4
Sparrowhawk	1 : 9.9 : 5.2	1 : 8.8 : 4.0
Kestrel	1 : 1.7 : 0.97	1 : 1.3 : 0.84
Barn owl	1 : 0.59 : 0.20	1 : 0.58 : 0.20

What then is the likely significance of the residue loads in these various species? Regarding lethal effects, authors have for many years held the view that, in Britain, cyclodienes have been the most harmful of the organochlorines. For instance, Mellanby (1967) concluded: "only very few birds seem to have high enough residues of DDT, DDE or BHC [hexachlorocyclohexane] for them to have been seriously damaged. On the other hand, dieldrin . . . . which is so much more poisonous to birds, has quite often been found at levels which are certainly harmful and are probably lethal". Assuming that minimum levels in the liver indicative of death by poisoning are: HEOD, 10 ppm; DDE, 100 ppm; PCBs, 100 ppm, HEOD made a much greater impact on kestrels and barn owls than did DDE or PCBs (Table 4). However, an appreciable number of kestrel and barn owl carcases had at least 10 ppm DDE or PCBs in the liver, and such levels may have caused other effects, such as shell thinning (see Ratcliffe 1970). It is perhaps naive to consider residues individually, as all three residues were present in virtually all samples, and there may have been an additive or synergistic effect. Looking at the significance of residues individually does at least have the advantage of erring on the side of caution, and, because little is known about additive or synergistic effects, this is the only feasible approach at present.

In sparrowhawk livers, HEOD residues of 10 or more ppm were comparatively rare (Table 4). If there are no interspecific differences in sensitivity, this observation may suggest that HEOD had relatively little impact on sparrowhawk mortality during the period 1963-1975. Interspecific differences in susceptibility cannot be discounted, however (see p.13), and it should be remembered that these carcases were collected *after* sparrowhawk populations had declined dramatically over much of England, allegedly because of cyclodiene poisoning (Prestt 1965). Concentrations of DDE or

PCBs of 10 or more ppm were commonly found in sparrowhawk livers, suggesting that sublethal effects may have been widespread. Indeed, a wide variety of reproductive defects attributable to DDE or PCBs has been reported for this species, including shell thinning, shell breakage and hatching failure (Ratcliffe 1970; Newton & Bogan 1974, 1978). A few sparrowhawk livers contained sufficient DDE to suggest that this pollutant may have caused death.

Moore and Walker (1964) found that heron muscle contained higher concentrations of HEOD and DDE than muscle from other species, and heron eggs contained the highest total organochlorine residues. From the material presented in Table 4, herons had the highest average concentration of DDE and PCBs. The ratios of mean levels were similar to those of sparrowhawks (Table 5), but the percentages of samples exceeding residue 'thresholds' of 10 or 100 ppm were consistently higher than the respective figures for sparrowhawks. One might imagine that the herons experience a certain degree of mortality due to HEOD (or DDE or PCBs), together with extensive sublethal effects. Certainly shell thinning and breakage occurred to a marked extent in some colonies (Prestt 1970; Cooke *et al.* 1976), but it is not known how widespread these phenomena were. Nor has much concern been expressed about the scale of death due to HEOD poisoning; possibly the lack of concern has stemmed from the fact that heron populations are not believed to have declined nationally because of environmental pollution.

Variations in organochlorine residue levels during the year

i. Number of carcases in each death category during the year: Numbers of carcases analysed in each month are shown in Figure 7 for the material collected up to 1975. Few carcases were obtained in the summer months. Samples in the trauma group were generally available throughout the year, except in mid-summer. Poor-condition kestrels were most numerous from August to December and were often juveniles. Carcases in the remainder groups were particularly numerous during the first four months of the year, and especially in March and April.

ii. Mean residues in livers for each month: Seasonal changes in residue levels were similar in all species, and three examples are given in Figures 8-10. Residues tended to rise to a peak in the spring or early summer, fell rapidly around July or August and then remained low for the rest of the year. Taking trauma and total samples of all species, the months during which maximum mean residues occurred were February (two occasions), March (1), April (7), May (8), June (5), November (1) (Table 6). There were no consistent overall trends for one pollutant residue to reach a peak earlier or later than either of the others. Residues

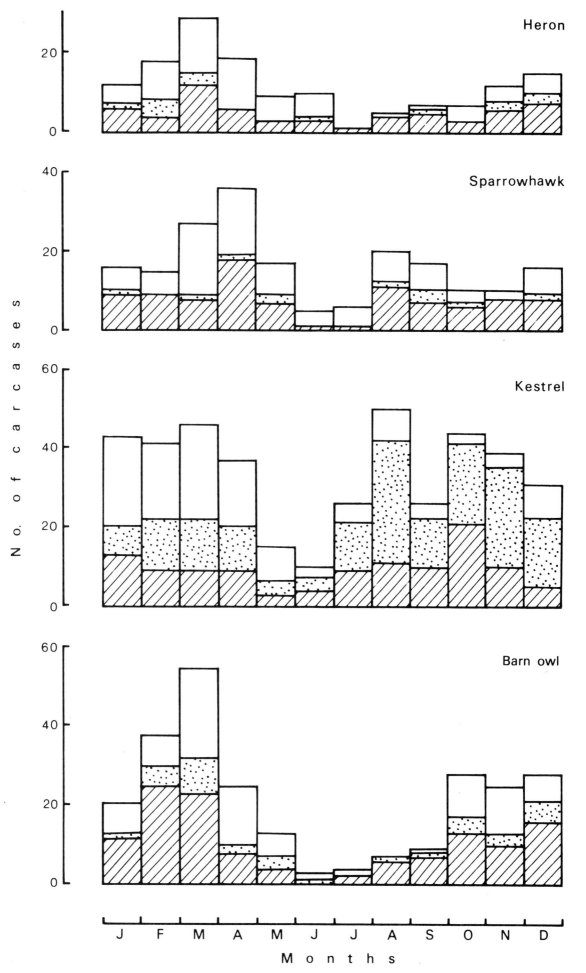

Figure 7.   Heron, sparrowhawk, kestrel and barn owl: monthly carcase numbers. Trauma (cross-hatched); poor-condition (stippled); remainder (unshaded).

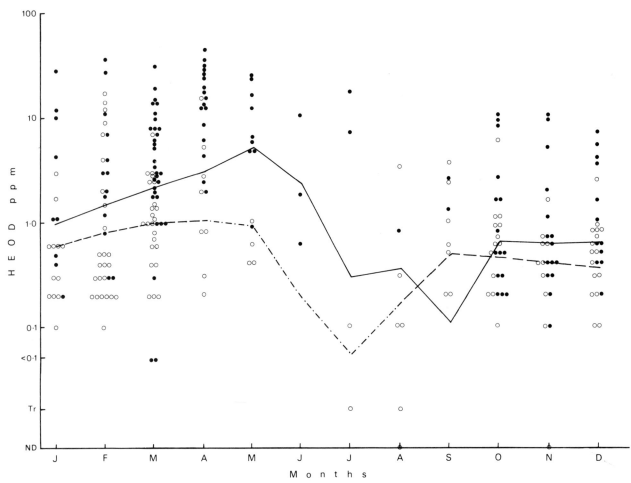

Figure 8.   *Barn owl: HEOD residues in livers month by month.* ○, *trauma;* ●, *non-trauma. 3-monthly trend of geometric means:* — — — —, *trauma;* — · — · —, *where 2-month values only available);* ————, *all samples.*

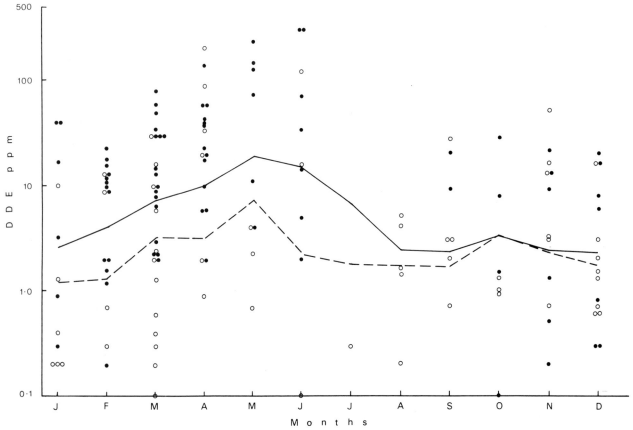

Figure 9.   *Heron: DDE residues in livers month by month.* ○, *trauma;* ●, *non-trauma. 3-monthly trend of geometric means:* — — — —, *trauma;* ————, *all samples.*

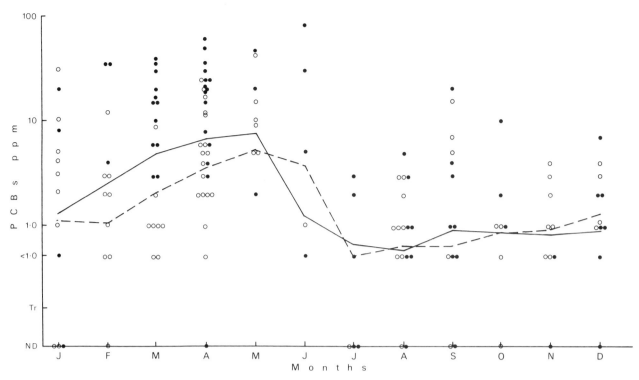

Figure 10. Sparrowhawk: PCB residues in livers month by month. ○, trauma; ●, non-trauma. 3-monthly trend of geometric means: — — —, trauma; ———, all samples.

tended to peak later in the year in sparrowhawks (May/June) than in barn owls (March/April), and sparrowhawks showed signs of a second (smaller) peak in mid-winter in HEOD and DDE. These trends were not simply the result of large numbers of juvenile birds tending to depress mean residues in the autumn. For instance, there were no significant differences in residue levels for adults and juveniles in the trauma group for the kestrel, and mean residues for the combined trauma group showed a peak in spring or early summer (Table 6). Bell and Murton (1977), using some of these data, demonstrated similar seasonal trends in HEOD residues in adult and juvenile kestrels.

iii. Numbers of samples with residues of 10 or more ppm during each quarter of the year: Many
liver samples had residues of 10 ppm or more. This was taken as a convenient level to indicate the seasonal distribution of carcasses with high liver residues. Seasonal changes are shown for the kestrel (Figure 11) as the percentage of samples during each quarter with at least 10 ppm of each residue. Generally maximum percentages tended to occur in the second quarter (ie April-June), whereas in both kestrels and sparrowhawks the greatest percentage of samples

with high HEOD concentrations occurred in the first quarter.

iv. Changes in residues in liver and fat, October-April:
In order to understand more about uptake and storage of residues within birds, liver and fat samples were analysed from some trauma birds collected during the autumn and spring, October-December and January-April (Table 7). The data suggested that, for the kestrel, levels were low in autumn in both fat and liver and increased in both tissues in the spring. Fewer samples were available for sparrowhawks and barn owls, but these seemed to follow the same trend. All the birds sampled had reasonable amounts of body fat.

v. Discussion.
Residues tended to be at their highest in the livers of dead birds during the spring or early summer. Why should such a cycle exist, and why should it be essentially the same for each of the pollutants studied? One might begin by examining seasonal changes in the availability of these materials in the environment. However, whereas HEOD may have been more available in autumn when the dressed grain should have been sown, DDT was presumably more commonly applied in the spring and summer

TABLE 6

Months in which geometric mean residues attained maximum values. These do not necessarily coincide exactly with the peaks shown by 3-monthly moving averages as in Figs 8-10.

	Trauma groups			Total samples		
	HEOD	DDE	PCBs	HEOD	DDE	PCBs
Heron	February	April	November	May	April	May
Sparrowhawk	May	May	May	June	June	May
Kestrel	May	June	June	February	June	May
Barn owl	April	March	April	April	April	April

TABLE 7

Geometric mean residues in liver and fat samples from trauma birds collected in autumn and spring.

			October–December		January–April
		n	Geometric mean (ppm) (range of values within 1 standard error)	n	Geometric mean (ppm) (range of values within 1 standard error)
HEOD					
Kestrel	Liver	11	0.45 (0.33–0.61)	12	1.28 (0.59–2.81)
	Fat	11	0.81 (0.52–1.25)	12	10.5*(4.76–23.0)
Sparrowhawk	Liver	1	Trace	6	0.33 (0.26–0.41)
	Fat	1	0.0	6	3.02 (2.27–4.03)
Barn owl	Liver	10	0.06 (0.02–0.13)	6	0.53 (0.32–0.87)
	Fat	10	1.42 (0.89–2.27)	6	4.25 (2.47–7.32)
DDE					
Kestrel	Liver	11	0.10 (0.04–0.22)	12	1.00*(0.73–1.36)
	Fat	11	4.53 (2.95–6.96)	12	27.3*(16.7–44.6)
Sparrowhawk	Liver	1	0.5	6	3.02 (2.27–4.03)
	Fat	1	5.0	6	54.0 (35.7–81.6)
Barn owl	Liver	10	0.05 (0.02–0.11)	6	0.39 (0.24–0.63)
	Fat	10	1.24 (0.80–1.93)	6	4.52 (2.92–6.99)
PCBs					
Kestrel	Liver	11	0.12 (0.06–0.25)	12	0.73*(0.56–0.98)
	Fat	11	2.79 (1.50–5.20)	12	11.9 (5.45–26.0)
Sparrowhawk	Liver	1	<1.0	6	1.91 (1.65–2.20)
	Fat	1	8.0	6	28.1 (18.3–43.2)
Barn owl	Liver	10	0.05 (0.03–0.11)	6	0.04 (0.02–0.08)
	Fat	10	1.06 (0.82–1.38)	6	1.20 (0.42–3.47)

Significantly different from mean of October-December, *, $P<0.05$

(eg see Moreton & Kite 1975), while there seems no reason to expect any particular seasonal peak in PCB availability. In other words, seasonal changes in liver pollutant levels did not appear to follow the expected seasonal changes in exposure. Similar trends were noted by Jones, Stanley, Summers and Wardall (in preparation), who shot and analysed blackbirds *(Turdus merula)* in an orchard area that had not been treated with DDT for several years. The kestrels, sparrowhawks and barn owls selected for analysis (Table 7) had ample fat and there was no indication of loss of fat during the period studied. Information is therefore consistent with an increase in total body burden of pollutants since concentrations increased in both fat and liver comparing the periods October-December with January-April.

Seasonal cycles in lipid levels do occur, however (eg see Hirons (1976) for tawny owls *(Strix aluco)*, Newton (1968) for bullfinches *(Pyrrhula pyrrhula)*, and Ward (1978) for starlings *(Sturnus vulgaris)*. Ward summarised the cycle in the starling thus: "Seasonal changes in lipid content were unexceptional for a temperate zone species. In January and February, the birds generally carried large reserves of fat — sufficient at least for metabolism during the long cold nights. The level was greatly reduced at the end of winter, and remained low throughout the summer and autumn."

There is no reason for supposing that the raptors would not fit into this same general pattern. We have limited information from visual assessments made of the amounts of body fat (none, little, moderate, much) on a number of carcases. In the trauma group for the kestrel (Figure 12), birds with moderate or large amounts of fat were more common in winter. Not one of the birds collected from April to June was classed as having much fat. Some fat loss was indicated during the spring, but this needs confirmation. However, it appears that after the body burden of fat-soluble residues begins to build up, the amount of depot fat decreases and liver residues rise (see Ecobichon & Saschenbrecker 1969). This association between fat mobilisation and increased liver residues has been demonstrated for the blackbird by Jones *et al.* (in preparation).

This hypothesis of an increase in the body burden of fat-soluble toxins followed by fat mobilisation would also explain why the liver levels of all three pollutants increase and reach a peak at about the same time. Body burdens of all residues appear to rise from around January (eg see Table 7). Thus, the peaks in liver residues of DDE and PCBs are not secondary effects in response to damage by HEOD to fat metabolism, ie it might have been suggested that birds dying from HEOD poisoning in the spring (see

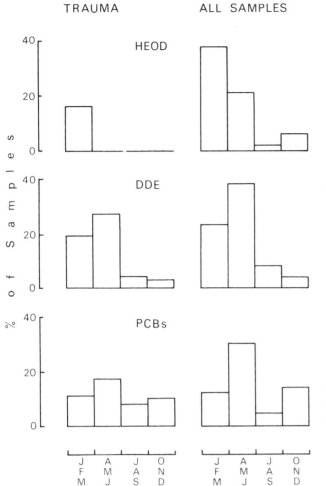

Figure 11. Kestrel: percentage of samples with liver residues of 10 or more ppm.

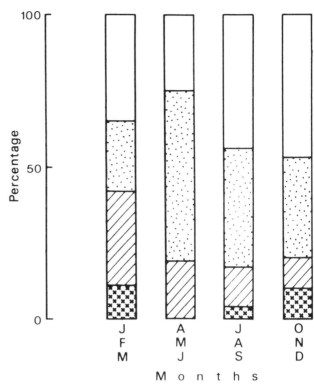

Figure 12. Kestrel: percentage of trauma birds found in each quarter of the year, according to amount of body fat. Much (heavy stipple); moderate (cross-hatched); little (light stipple); none (unshaded).

Figure 7) suffered fat mobilisation and this resulted in elevated levels of DDE and PCBs in the liver, as well as higher levels of HEOD. However, HEOD poisoning, and to a lesser extent DDE poisoning, presumably provided additional impetus to the lipid mobilisation that occurs naturally at that time of year. Possible reasons for an increase in body burden towards the spring include: (1) a switch in choice or availability of prey items towards more contaminated prey; (2) an increase in the amount of food consumed; or (3) an increase in the amount of organochlorine absorbed through the gut wall or retained in the body. Ward (1979) has demonstrated that waders acquire high concentrations of zinc prior to their pre-nuptial moult, and at the same time take up (apparently incidentally) high concentrations of cadmium and mercury. This increase is accomplished without a change of diet.

Carcases in the remainder groups were collected mainly during the first four months of the year, and especially in March and April (Figure 7). After it was appreciated that the mass deaths of birds during the spring months (from 1956 to 1961) could be attributed to cyclodiene ingestion, there was a tendency to blame suspected poisoning incidents in the spring on the late sowing of grain dressed for winter use (see also Bailey et al. 1974). Now that some information is

available on seasonal cycles of tissue toxins, one must conclude that physiological factors were also likely to be implicated to some extent in the trend for poisoning incidents to occur mainly in spring.

Seasonal changes must be taken into account in any monitoring programme (Figures 8-10). For instance, if carcases of a species happen to be collected during the spring of one year and the autumn of the next, there may well be a significant decrease in liver residues in the second year, due solely to the seasonal effect. It may be better in future to collect and analyse only birds killed during the first six months of the year. These will tend to have high residues and should reflect annual or geographical trends in levels at least as well as samples collected throughout the year.

An incident that was in the news is relevant here. Staff of the Zoological Society of London had been alarmed by the deaths of many owls in their collection: 55 individuals of 21 species died between March 1974 and September 1976 (Jones et al. 1978). At least 28 of these owls were in good condition and death was eventually found to be due to HEOD poisoning. Mice, used as food, had been kept on sawdust previously treated with dieldrin, and had passed on lethal residues to the owls. Of these 28 owls, 20 died during the first four months of 1976 and no less than 15 died during April. This is the month when barn owls are at greatest risk from HEOD poisoning (Table 6). It seems that other species of owl (like the other birds studied in this report) may have similar seasonal cycles. Another incident involving the deaths of seabirds in Los

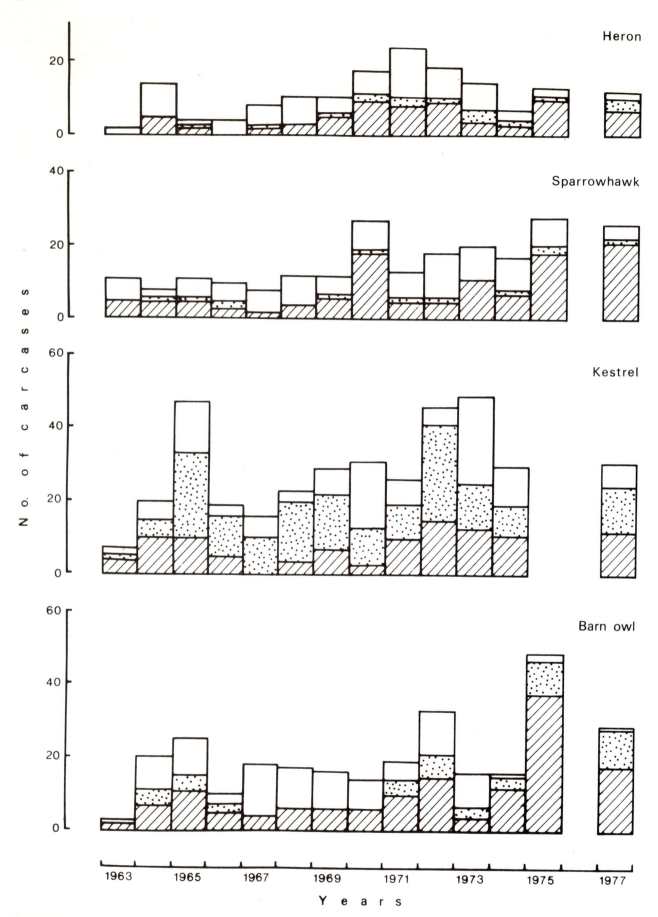

Figure 13. Number of carcases according to category of death year by year: Trauma (cross-hatched); poor-condition (stippled); remainder (unshaded). Analyses were restricted to carcases obtained in part of the year only for kestrels in 1975, and for all four species in 1976: data for these years are omitted.

Angeles County Zoo in the "early summer of 1976" was reported by Clark (1978).

Annual variations in organochlorine residue levels

i. Number of carcases in each death category during each year: Numbers of carcases analysed in each year are shown in Figure 13. Over this time span, there were no marked changes in the relative proportions in the different death categories that were consistent for all four species. During recent years, however, trauma birds in heron and barn owl seemed to increase at the expense of remainder birds.

ii. Mean residues in livers for each year: The main aim was to find whether the restrictions in organochlorine use over the years did affect the residue levels found in wildlife samples. Although all our samples were analysed in the same laboratory, occasional changes in analyst or technique may have introduced some extra variability, and it is well to bear this in mind when assessing long-term trends.

Annual mean residues of HEOD, DDE and PCBs were calculated for the trauma group and for total samples of each species. In the previous section, it was reported that liver residues tended to be higher during the first six months of the year. Because the missing analyses from 1975 and 1976 all came from the

second half of the year, inclusion of the available analytical figures would presumably give artificially high mean values: means for 1975 and 1976 are therefore omitted when appropriate.

No clear consistent trend emerged for mean HEOD levels. In barn owls (shown as an example in Figure 14) and kestrels, residues fluctuated but showed no tendency to decline, at least up to 1973/74, despite the withdrawal of dieldrin from certain uses. The total samples for the heron and barn owl displayed two peaks, the first during 1967/1968 and the second around 1972/73. HEOD residues in herons in the 1970s were lower than they had been in the 1960s; those in sparrowhawks appeared to decrease somewhat earlier. Mean residues for all species were low in 1977.

Overall, DDE residues were much the same in the early 1970s as they had been in the mid-1960s (eg see barn owl Figure 15 and kestrel Figure 16), but, between these periods, species tended to show a peak in mean residues. These peaks were several years apart in different species: in 1970, residues in kestrel samples were high, but in barn owl samples were low. If DDE figures had a bias towards high residues in one or more years because of changes in laboratory techniques, then the changes in mean residues would be expected to coincide more closely.

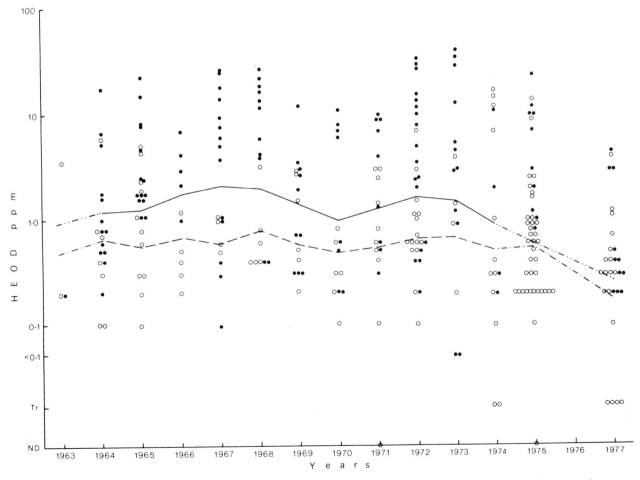

Figure 14. Barn owl: HEOD residues in livers year by year: ○, trauma; ●, non-trauma. 3-yearly trend of geometric means: — — — —, trauma (— · — · —, where 2-year values only available); —————, all samples (—··—··).

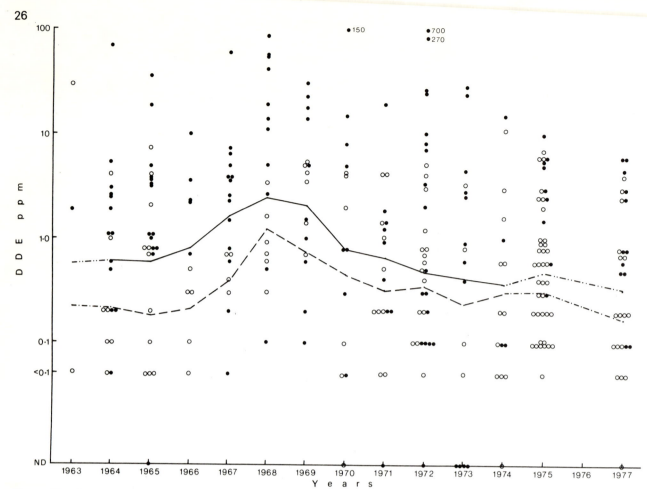

Figure 15. Barn owl: DDE residues in livers year by year. ○, trauma; ●, non-trauma. 3-yearly trend of geometric means: — — — —, trauma (— · — · — ·, where 2-year values only available); ————, all samples (—·—··).

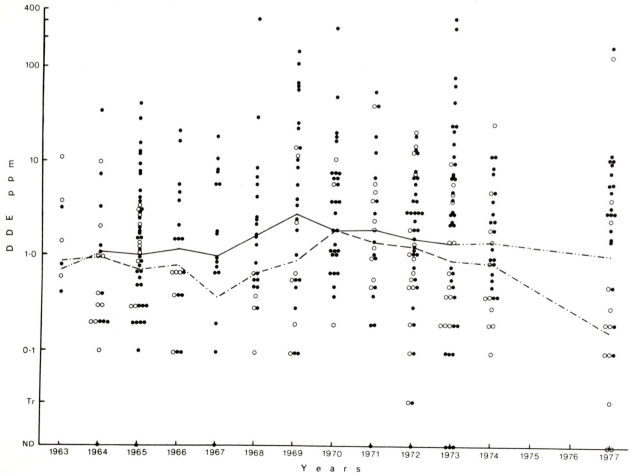

Figure 16. Kestrel: DDE residues in livers year by year. ○, trauma; ●, non-trauma. 3-yearly trend of geometric means: — — — —, trauma (— · — · — ·, where 2-year values only available); ————, all samples (—··—··—).

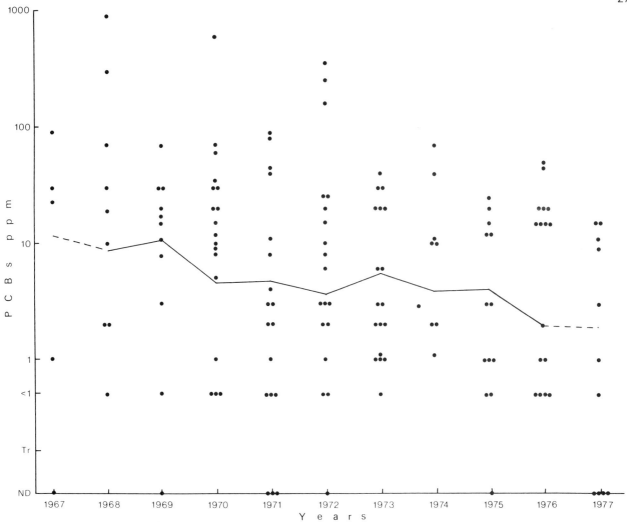

Figure 17. Heron: PCB residues in livers year by year. Death categories are not distinguished because of small samples. •, all samples. 3-yearly trend of geometric means: ——— (— — — —, where 2-year values only available).

Residues of PCBs fluctuated widely for the four species, and in no consistent pattern. However, for herons (Figure 17), kestrels, and barn owls, mean residues during the 1970s seemed lower than they had been during the late 1960s.

iii. The effect of the withdrawal of organochlorines on liver residue: The 15 years, from 1963 to 1977, can be divided into four periods according to organochlorine usage.

a. 1963-1965. From 1961, there had been a voluntary ban on the spring sowing of grain treated with aldrin or dieldrin. Even by 1963, pollution from this source should have diminished from the level attained in the late 1950s (see Robinson 1967). Some of the recommendations of the Cook Report (1964) were implemented in 1965. This period is the baseline for the purposes of this survey.

b. 1966-1971. In 1966, dieldrin was banned from use in sheep dips. There were no restrictions on the uses of DDT in agriculture, but, because of the Cook recommendations (1964), cyclodiene concentrations in wildlife samples might have been expected to decrease compared with the previous period (eg see Coulson *et al.* 1972).

c. 1972-1975. Some uses of DDT and dieldrin were phased out from 1972 in accordance with the recom-

mendations of the Wilson Report (1969). Dieldrin was still being used as a seed dressing in the autumn and winter. In 1971, Monsanto withdrew PCBs from uses where they were most likely to contaminate the environment.

d. 1977. Dieldrin was no longer used as a seed dressing, but dieldrin and DDT still had a variety of insecticidal uses in industry and agriculture.

In the following statistical analyses, mean residues for one period are tested against the mean for the previous period. Means and statistical details are presented in Tables 8-10.

For HEOD residues (Table 8), there were no statistically significant changes in herons, kestrels or barn owls until 1977, when mean liver residues decreased; in herons, the mean for the total samples tended to decrease progressively from 1963 to 1965. In sparrowhawks, the main decrease occurred during the period 1966-1971.

DDE residues showed a very different pattern to those of HEOD (Table 9). The only occasions that statistical differences were observed involved an increase to a maximum at the end of the 1960s in kestrels (see Figure 16), and a decrease from this period in herons

TABLE 8

Geometric mean of HEOD residues in the livers of herons, sparrowhawks, kestrels and barn owls in different periods.

		Heron			Sparrowhawk			Kestrel			Barn owl	
		Geometric mean (ppm) (range of values within			Geometric mean (ppm) (range of values within			Geometric mean (ppm) (range of values within			Geometric mean (ppm) (range of values within	
	n	1 standard error)		n	1 standard error)		n	1 standard error)		n	1 standard error)	
Trauma												
1963-65	7	0.09 (0.03–0.31)		15	0.80 (0.58–1.09)		24	0.78 (0.67–0.91)		20	0.67 (0.49–0.90)	
		$t_{32}=0.966$			$t_{47}=2.935$	D**		$t_{46}=1.952$			$t_{55}=0.596$	
1966-71	27	0.28 (0.17–0.48)		38	0.19 (0.13–0.28)		29	0.45 (0.35–0.57)		37	0.53 (0.42–0.67)	
		$t_{51}=0.086$			$t_{77}=1.204$			$t_{66}=1.549$			$t_{104}=0.130$	
1972-75	26	0.30 (0.21–0.44)		41	0.35 (0.25–0.48)		39	0.80 (0.61–1.04)		69	0.55 (0.45–0.68)	
		$t_{31}=1.569$			$t_{60}=1.188$			$t_{49}=2.752$	D**		$t_{85}=2.608$	D**
1977	7	0.07 (0.02–0.22)		21	0.18 (0.12–0.28)		12	0.15 (0.08–0.30)		18	0.16 (0.10–0.26)	
Total												
1963-65	26	1.13 (0.66–1.94)		30	1.20 (0.97–1.49)		74	1.09 (0.94–1.27)		48	1.31 (1.08–1.60)	
		$t_{43}=0.341$			$t_{102}=41.27$	D***		$t_{198}=0.136$			$t_{140}=0.270$	
1966-71	69	0.92 (0.67–1.26)		82	0.29 (0.22–0.38)		144	1.06 (0.91–1.24)		94	1.42 (1.19–1.69)	
		$t_{123}=0.529$			$t_{163}=2.048$	I*		$t_{267}=1.232$			$t_{206}=1.098$	
1972-75	57	0.74 (0.57–0.96)		83	0.61 (0.48–0.78)		125	1.43 (1.19–1.72)		114	1.07 (0.90–1.28)	
		$t_{67}=2.224$	D*		$t_{107}=2.157$	D*		$t_{154}=3.682$	D***		$t_{141}=3.603$	D***
1977	12	0.17 (0.08–0.37)		26	0.22 (0.15–0.32)		31	0.31 (0.21–0.45)		29	0.26 (0.18–0.37)	

t-test: significantly different, *, $P<0.05$; **, $P<0.01$; ***, $P<0.001$. I=increase; D=decrease.
degrees of freedom were calculated using the formula given in Bailey (1959) for the comparison of means of two samples where the variances were unequal.

and barn owls. Residues in 1977 were not significantly lower than those found during 1972-1975. Samples for herons, kestrels and barn owls showed a progressive decrease in mean DDE residues from the period 1966-1971.

As regards PCB residues (Table 10), the sparrowhawk again differed from the others in that it showed no significant decrease in liver residues over the years. The kestrel and barn owl showed a significant decline in residues following the ban on PCBs in 1971, though in the barn owl the main decrease occurred in 1970, before the ban was introduced. Residues in herons declined significantly in 1977 and in total samples showed a general downward trend throughout the period under review.

TABLE 9

Geometric mean of DDE residues in the livers of herons, sparrowhawks, kestrels and barn owls in different periods.

		Heron			Sparrowhawk			Kestrel			Barn owl	
		Geometric mean (ppm) (range of values within			Geometric mean (ppm) (range of values within			Geometric mean (ppm) (range of values within			Geometric mean (ppm) (range of values within	
	n	1 standard error)		n	1 standard error)		n	1 standard error)		n	1 standard error)	
Trauma												
1963-65	7	2.53 (1.33–4.82)		15	4.14 (2.83–6.06)		24	1.01 (0.78–1.30)		20	0.22 (0.12–1.41)	
		$t_{32}=0.447$			$t_{51}=0.126$			$t_{51}=0.322$			$t_{55}=0.955$	
1966-71	27	3.69 (2.49–5.48)		38	3.90 (3.04–5.01)		29	1.15 (0.85–1.54)		37	0.42 (0.29–0.42)	
		$t_{51}=1.948$			$t_{77}=1.516$			$t_{66}=0.504$			$t_{104}=0.592$	
1972-75	26	1.40 (1.04–1.89)		41	2.21 (1.67–2.92)		39	0.93 (0.70–1.23)		69	0.33 (0.26–0.42)	
		$t_{31}=0.046$			$t_{60}=0.885$			$t_{13}=1.689$			$t_{85}=1.293$	
1977	7	1.36 (0.70–2.63)		21	3.29 (2.40–4.51)		12	0.16 (0.06–0.44)		18	0.16 (0.09–0.29)	
Total												
1963-65	26	7.75 (5.69–10.6)		30	5.41 (4.16–7.03)		74	1.06 (0.86–1.32)		48	0.61 (0.42–0.88)	
		$t_{93}=0.133$			$t_{110}=0.687$			$t_{216}=2.519$	I*		$t_{140}=1.406$	
1966-71	69	8.23 (6.40–10.6)		82	4.15 (3.36–5.13)		144	2.14 (1.81–2.52)		94	1.13 (0.88–1.46)	
		$t_{122}=3.397$	D***		$t_{163}=0.176$			$t_{267}=1.597$			$t_{206}=2.344$	D*
1972-75	56	2.69 (2.18–3.32)		83	4.38 (3.39–5.55)		125	1.42 (1.16–1.73)		114	0.50 (0.39–0.64)	
		$t_{66}=1.125$			$t_{107}=0.125$			$t_{154}=0.606$			$t_{141}=0.896$	
1977	12	1.54 (1.00–2.36)		26	4.15 (2.92–5.87)		31	1.06 (0.63–1.77)		29	0.32 (0.21–0.48)	

t-test: significantly different, *, $P<0.05$; ***, $P<0.001$. I=increase; D=decrease.
degrees of freedom were calculated using the formula given in Bailey (1959) for the comparison of means of two samples where the variances were unequal.

TABLE 10

Geometric mean of PCB residues in the livers of herons, sparrowhawks, kestrels and barn owls in different periods.

		Heron			Sparrowhawk			Kestrel				Barn owl	
	n	Geometric mean (ppm) (range of values within 1 standard error)		n	Geometric mean (ppm) (range of values within 1 standard error)		n	Geometric mean (ppm) (range of values within 1 standard error)			n	Geometric mean (ppm) (range of values within 1 standard error)	
Trauma													
1967-71	26	2.27 (1.34–3.84)		35	1.59 (1.13–2.24)		24	0.88 (0.58–1.34)			30	0.15 (0.09–0.25)	
		$t_{42}=0.225$			$t_{74}=0.022$			$t_{59}=1.236$				$t_{97}=0.849$	
1972-75	26	2.61 (1.88–3.64)		41	1.61 (1.18–2.19)		37	0.38 (0.23–0.61)			69	0.09 (0.07–0.13)	
		$t_{7}=1.540$			$t_{57}=0.301$			$t_{47}=1.399$				$t_{85}=0.632$	
1977	7	0.34 (0.09–1.22)		21	1.82 (1.38–2.41)		12	0.10 (0.05–0.21)			18	0.06 (0.04–0.11)	
Total													
1967-71	62	5.77 (4.13–8.05)		70	1.74 (1.33–2.26)		116	1.57 (1.29–1.92)			76	0.44 (0.32–0.59)	
		$t_{113}=0.628$			$t_{151}=0.773$			$t_{236}=3.031$	D**			$t_{188}=2.284$	D*
1972-75	57	4.41 (3.39–5.75)		83	2.29 (1.80–2.92)		125	0.62 (0.49–0.78)			114	0.17 (0.13–0.22)	
		$t_{13}=2.177$	D*		$t_{107}=0.605$			$t_{154}=0.049$				$t_{141}=0.245$	
1977	12	0.56 (0.23–1.40)		26	1.72 (1.25–2.37)		31	0.60 (0.39–0.93)			29	0.15 (0.09–0.23)	

t-test: significantly different, *, $P<0.05$; **, $P<0.01$. D=decrease.
   degrees of freedom were calculated using the formula given in Bailey (1959) for the comparison of means of two samples where the variances were unequal.

iv. Samples with residues of 10 ppm or more, or 100 ppm or more, during each period:

Many liver samples still had 10 ppm or more HEOD during the period 1972-75 (Table 11). Indeed in sparrowhawks, kestrels and barn owls there was a steady rise from the 1963-65 period in the percentage of liver samples with such high HEOD residues. In 1977, however, not one of the overall total of 98 livers had a HEOD concentration of 10 ppm.

The peak in mean DDE concentrations near the end of the 1960s was reflected in the consistently high percentages of samples with at least 10 ppm DDE during 1966-1971. After that time, percentages dropped steadily in herons and barn owls and to a lesser extent in sparrowhawks, but stayed more or less constant in kestrels. Overall, the decrease from 1966-1971 to 1972-1975 was highly significant. Unlike HEOD and PCBs, DDE residues failed to show a significant reduction for all species in 1977.

None of the four species showed any appreciable changes in the percentages of livers with 10 ppm or more PCBs from 1967-1971 to 1972-1975. In 1977, however, the percentage dropped for all four species; all of the kestrel and barn owl livers (n=60) had less

TABLE 11

Percentage of liver samples with different residue levels (ppm) in different periods.

	1963-1965		1966-1971[†]		1972-1975		1977	
	%≥10	%≥100	%≥10	%≥100	%≥10	%≥100	%≥10	%≥100
HEOD								
Heron	15	0	19	0	7	0	0	0
Sparrowhawk	3	0	5	0	10	0	0	0
Kestrel	8	0	17	0	24	0	0	0
Barn owl	6	0	15	0	18	0	0	0
ALL 4 SPECIES	8	0	14*	0	16	0	0***	0
DDE								
Heron	50	4	55	10	29	0	17	0
Sparrowhawk	30	3	37	2	36	6	27	4
Kestrel	11	0	19	3	17	2	19	7
Barn owl	8	0	17	1	9	2	0	0
ALL 4 SPECIES	19	1	29*	4	20**	2	15	3
PCBs								
Heron			52	5	42	5	25	0
Sparrowhawk			24	0	27	0	15	0
Kestrel			16	1	11	0	0	0
Barn owl			9	0	10	0	0	0
ALL 4 SPECIES			23	1	19	1	7**	0

† for PCBs the period started in 1967.
χ^2 test for all 4 species: significantly different from previous period, *, $P<0.05$; **, $P<0.01$; ***, $P<0.001$.

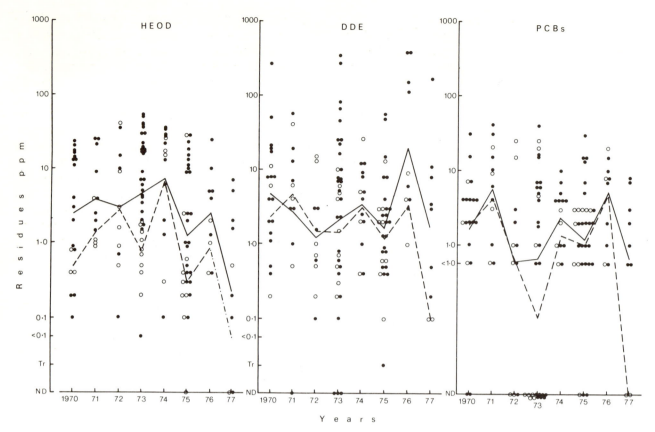

Figure 18. *Kestrel, 1970-1977: residues in the livers of carcases collected during the period January-June. 3-yearly trend of geometric means: — — — —, trauma; ————, all samples.*

than 10 ppm. Overall, the decrease was statistically significant.

v. Mean residue levels in the livers of kestrels collected during the first half of each year: As stated above, in 1975 and 1976 kestrel livers were analysed only from the first half of the year, a time at which residues tend to be high. In retrospect, this was unfortunate since dieldrin was withdrawn finally from use as a seed dressing at the end of 1975. We therefore calculated the mean residues for the samples collected during the first six months of each year in the period 1970-1977 (Figure 18). The figures for HEOD suggest that the large decrease (as reported in Table 8) preceded the final withdrawal by one year. The decrease in HEOD concentration from 1974 to 1975 was statistically significant (all samples: $t_{43}=2.54$, $P<0.05$). The mean HEOD residues calculated for 1975, 1976 and 1977 were all relatively low.

In the figure, there was a peak for mean DDE in the total sample in 1976. The rise in DDE levels from 1975 to 1976 was significant ($t_{39}=3.60$; $P<0.001$), as was the decrease from 1976 to 1977 ($t_{17}=2.21$, $P<0.05$). Mean PCB residues fell from 1971, then increased to 1976 and finally decreased again in 1977. The increase for PCBs in 1976 was not statistically significant.

vi. Discussion: Despite the various restrictions imposed upon the uses of aldrin and dieldrin, residues of HEOD in kestrel and barn owl livers showed little change up to about 1974 or 1975 (Figure 14, Table 8).

During the period 1972-75, 62 (16%) liver samples out of a total of 379 for the four species contained at least 10 ppm HEOD (Table 11), a level that may be indicative of death by HEOD poisoning. Among the kestrels during this period, one liver in every four had an HEOD concentration of 10 ppm or more. In 1977, however, not one sample in any of the species exceeded 10 ppm HEOD and mean residues had decreased from the previous period, often significantly (Tables 8 and 11). Data for the kestrel from the first six months of the year indicated that the decrease in HEOD content had occurred by 1975 (Figure 18), although the final ban did not come into operation until the end of that year. Mean residues for the barn owl decreased sharply, but not significantly, from a peak in 1973 (Figure 14).

To summarise, although the heron and sparrowhawk showed some earlier decreases in HEOD levels, residues generally did not fall markedly until the mid-1970s; by 1977 they were relatively low in all four species.

For many years, the Pest Infestation Control Laboratory (PICL) of MAFF has conducted an investigation of wildlife incidents attributable to agricultural chemicals. This scheme can be regarded as complementing the monitoring programme at Monks Wood. The percentage of the total number of incidents recorded each year believed to have involved dieldrin (HEOD) is shown in Figure 19 for the period 1964-1976. The percentages were calculated from material listed in the PICL Report for 1974-1976 (Anon 1978). As can be seen, up to the early 1970s there was no sign of any reduction in the percentage of incidents attributable to HEOD (about 20% per annum). The percentage was low in 1974 and 1975 and decreased further after then. In 1977, no incidents (out of 171) could be ascribed to HEOD poisoning (P. Stanley pers. comm.). These trends fitted those shown by pesticide residues in the monitoring programme and supported the conclusions on changes in residue levels and their significance.

The most obvious feature of the trends in DDE residues was the peak which appeared during the period 1967-1971 (eg Figures 15, 16 and Table 11). Mean residues in 1977 were often lower than they had been during 1972-1975, but none of the differences was significant (Table 9, and also Table 11). Overall, a decrease in DDE residues was apparent from the period 1966-1971 to 1977. In the PICL scheme, the percentage of wildlife incidents attributed each year to DDT fluctuated between 0 and 18% (Figure 19). Most of the victims were song birds poisoned in orchard incidents (see Anon 1978). The percentage of incidents attributed to DDT rose to a maximum in 1967; each year from 1966 to 1969 this was greater than 10%. This peak in incidents corresponded reasonably well with the peak in residues found in the monitoring programme. Since then, incidents attributed to DDT exceeded 10% only during one year (1972) and had decreased to 1% by 1977 (P. Stanley personal comm.). Why DDT/DDE incidents and residues should have been high in the late 1960s is not

clear, but presumably usage was heavier then. Since that time, there have been decreases in residues (Figure 16, Table 9) which may, in part, have stemmed from the implementation of restrictions recommended in the Wilson Report in 1969.

Returning to the investigation organised by PICL, the report of many deaths of immigrant birds due to DDE poisoning during the early months of 1976 was of particular interest (Anon 1978). Nine percent of the incidents in 1976 was attributed to DDT (Figure 19). Many of these birds were kestrels and the liver samples of the Monks Wood kestrels also showed a massive peak in DDE in 1976 (Figure 18). Again, the two schemes, one looking at numbers of incidents, the other at residue levels, complement each other to an extent that is reassuring.

PCB residues for the four species showed no consistent trends. Again, trends for the kestrel and barn owl were the most similar. Kestrel residues showed a peak in 1970 or 1971 and thereafter declined (Figure 18, Table 10). Monsanto introduced their ban in 1971, so there was an association in time between restriction in use and a decrease in residues. Levels in barn owls, however, declined before the ban was implemented. Residues in herons tended to show a general downward trend with time, while those in sparrowhawks showed no clear trend at all (Table 10). Residues in 1977 were generally lower than those found previously (Tables 10, 11).

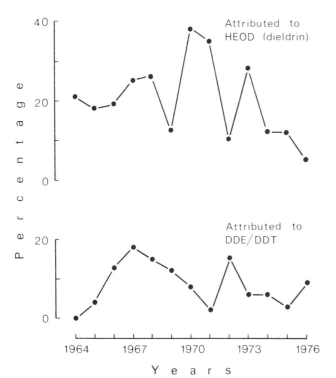

Figure 19. Summary of the 'Incident Scheme' organised by PICL: percentage of the total number of incidents for each year attributed to HEOD and DDE/DDT. (Graphs constructed from data in Anon 1978).

Variations in organochlorine residue levels between geographical regions

i. HEOD residues in relation to areas of attack by wheat bulb fly: Birds are thought to have acquired HEOD residues from aldrin and dieldrin, principally when these insecticides were used as seed dressings. So sedentary species living on farmland might be expected to have had higher residues in those areas where cyclodiene seed dressings were used in the largest amounts. It is probably reasonable to assume that areas known to suffer most acutely from attack by wheat bulb fly will have been treated most intensively with these chemicals. In this section, an attempt is made to compare, for each species, residues inside the main 'wheat bulb fly areas' with those in the rest of Britain. The heron is included because some of its HEOD load may have come from agriculture (Prestt 1970). Wheat bulb fly areas were delineated by Bell (1975), based on studies by Gough (1957).

Two maps are presented for each species (Figures 20-23). The maps on the left depict the distribution and magnitude of residues found in the trauma groups, while those on the right show organochlorine levels in the remainder groups. The remainder groups were used because they tended to contain the birds with high residues and might be expected to accentuate

TABLE 12

Numbers of samples with HEOD residues of certain size inside and outside areas prone to attack from wheat bulb fly (WBF). For each species, trauma groups and remainder groups are examined separately. Data abstracted from Figures 20-23

	Trauma group				Remainder group			
	0–0.9	1–9.9	≥10	Total	0–0.9	1–9.9	≥10	Total
Heron								
outside WBF areas	24	8	2	34	13	19	3	35
inside WBF areas	20	5	1	26	9	10	14	33**
Sparrowhawk								
outside WBF areas	53	26		79	42	27	6	75
inside WBF areas	4		1	5[NT]		2	5	7[NT]
Kestrel								
outside WBF areas	52	14	1	67	20	23	10	53
inside WBF areas	10	16	4	30***	5	14	44	63***
Barn owl								
outside WBF areas	52	12	1	65	21	18	13	52
inside WBF areas	32	21	3	56**	7	17	14	38***

** significantly greater proportion of high residues inside WBF areas, P<0.01; ***, P<0.001. [NT]=not tested, sample size too small.

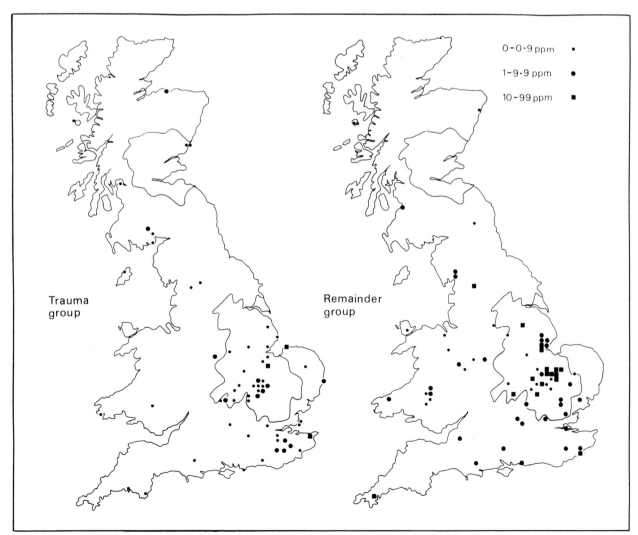

Figure 20. Heron: HEOD residues in livers; locations of samples from trauma and remainder groups. The two main areas of wheat bulb fly attack are shown.

any differences that existed between regions. Data are presented for the period 1963-1975, but exclude Ireland and the Channel Islands, for which there were few records.

Regional differences in residue levels were found, with the wheat bulb fly areas frequently containing a significantly greater proportion of samples with higher residues than elsewhere (Table 12). Only the trauma group for herons (Figure 20) failed to show this trend to some degree, though in the remainder group of this species the difference was highly significant. The heron trauma group consisted largely of birds collected during winter (Figure 7), and these may have been migrants from other parts of Britain or from the continent. So this group may be relatively poor for showing regional differences. On the other hand, many of the herons in the remainder group were collected during the breeding season (which in this species coincides with the seasonal peak in HEOD residues).

During the period studied, sparrowhoawks (Figure 21) were rare in eastern England, and too few birds were obtained for contingency testing. Nevertheless, the trend for a greater proportion of samples to have high

residues in the wheat bulb fly areas seemed to hold in this species too. In the wheat bulb fly areas, 6 (50%) out of 12 samples had HEOD residues of 10 or more ppm, while in the rest of the country 6 (4%) samples out of 154 had residues of this magnitude.

The regional differences in kestrels were most striking (Figure 22, Table 12). It is also interesting to note the relative numbers of birds in the trauma and remainder groups inside and outside the wheat bulb fly areas. For the trauma group, there were more than twice as many samples outside the wheat bulb fly areas as inside, but, for the remainder group, samples within the wheat bulb fly areas outnumbered those from elsewhere. This change, which was significant ($\chi^2=11.8$, $P<0.001$), was presumably due to an appreciable number of birds dying from dieldrin poisoning in the wheat bulb fly areas, thereby swelling the number from those areas in the remainder group.

In the barn owl remainder group, the trend for higher residues to occur in the wheat bulb fly areas was not quite significant, although there was a significant tendency for a greater proportion of HEOD residues of 10 or more ppm to be in those areas than elsewhere ($\chi^2=4.90$, $P<0.05$). In fact, almost all the samples with

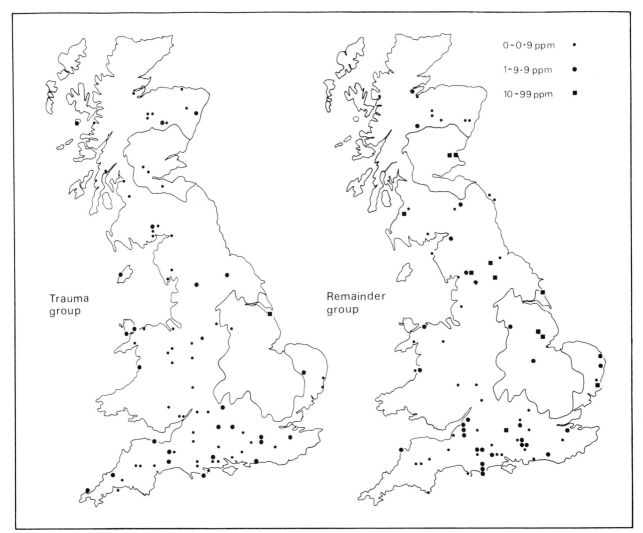

Figure 21. Sparrowhawk: HEOD residues in livers; locations of samples from trauma and remainder groups. The two main areas of wheat bulb fly attack are shown.

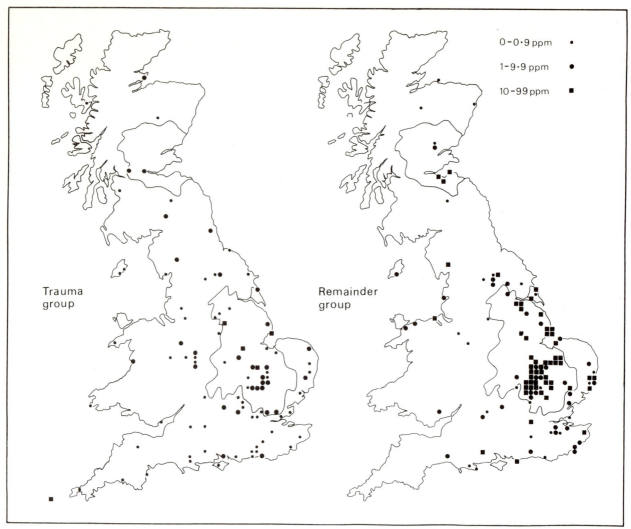

Figure 22. Kestrel: HEOD residues in livers; locations of samples from trauma and remainder groups. The two main areas of wheat bulb fly attack are shown.

high residues (10 ppm or more HEOD) for the remainder group were in eastern England (inside or just outside the wheat bulb fly area) or on the Isle of Man (Figure 23).

ii. Geographical variations in mean residue levels of HEOD, DDE and PCBs:

For the purpose of determining geographical variations in mean residue levels of HEOD, DDE and PCBs, Britain was divided into a number of regions (refer to Figure 24). First, North, West and East regions were demarcated. The East region included the main area of wheat bulb fly attack in England. There were no centres of wheat bulb fly attack in the West region. In the West region, the amounts of cyclodiene and other organochlorine insecticides used in agriculture should have been much lower than in the East (Cook 1964). The North region (N) included a centre of wheat bulb fly attack, where a certain amount of cyclodiene usage was to be expected. Statistical analysis for this region, however, suffers from the fact that few bird carcases were received.

Because many herons, kestrels and barn owls were analysed from the East region and because intra-regional variations might be expected, this region was

further divided into four parts (E1, E2, E3, E4 in Figure 24). It then became possible to test whether DDE residues were high in birds from the orchard-growing area of south-east England (for details and discussion, see Cook 1964; Mellanby 1967). Fewer samples were available for the West region, which was therefore divided only into two parts (W1 and W2). The study of Prestt *et al.* (1970) on PCBs revealed that carcases with high residues were widely distributed throughout Britain. High residues were found in birds frequenting diverse terrestrial and freshwater habitats and were not restricted to samples taken near industrial areas (see also Moriarty 1975). So, when considering PCBs, there was no reason to divide Britain in any particular manner in order to check previous statements.

Geometric mean residues are given in Tables 13, 14 and 15 for the seven regions for the trauma group and for total samples of each species. Within any one of these regional samples, there tended to be a considerable range of residue levels, and, for the trauma groups at least, the sample size was sometimes small; standard errors were correspondingly relatively large. No marked differences were apparent between geographical trends in residue levels shown by herons and those shown by the three terrestrial species. There-

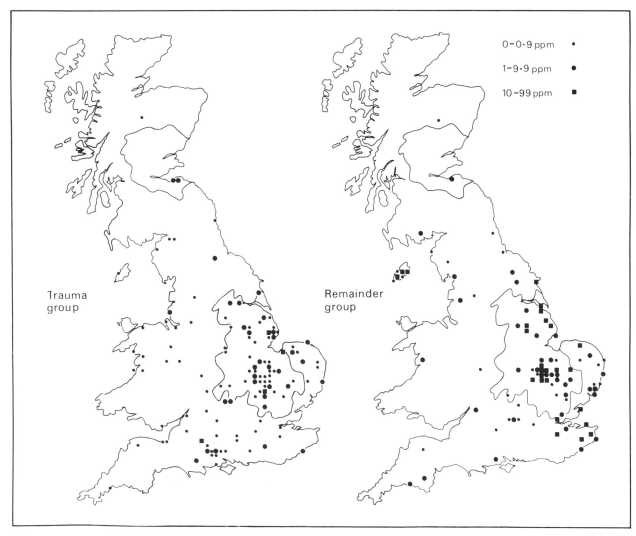

Figure 23. *Barn owl: HEOD residues in livers; locations of samples from trauma and remainder groups. The two main areas of wheat bulb fly attack are shown.*

fore, an overall assessment of relative residue levels in each area was made for the four species as follows. A scoring system was used whereby for any organochlorine/species combination the region with the highest mean residue was awarded a score of seven, the next highest was awarded six, and so on, until the lowest received a score of one. Scoring was done separately for the trauma groups and for total samples. For each region, the mean score for all four species was calculated, and, if the mean score was five or higher, the region was arbitrarily said to have 'high' residues; if three or lower, then 'low' residues; and between three and five, 'medium' residues (see Figure 24).

For each of the residues, there was good agreement between scores derived from trauma groups and those from total samples. The presence of such high residues of HEOD in samples from region E1 was somewhat surprising, bearing in mind the extent of the defined English wheat bulb fly problem. In fact, there were few samples from this region, but these tended to contain HEOD residues of at least comparable magnitude to those from E2 and E3, the regions covering the main wheat bulb fly problem. The importance of regions E1, E2 and E3 was shown

especially by data for kestrels and barn owls (Table 13), the species that tended overall to have the highest HEOD residues. Presumably, these species were more likely to encounter HEOD originating from application of seed dressings than were herons and sparrowhawks.

The highest residues of DDE were found consistently in regions E3 and E4 (Table 14, Figure 24). Thus, within the East region the pattern of variation of DDE residues was different from that of HEOD. Samples collected from region E4 tended to have the highest mean residues of DDE, but only low or medium residues of HEOD.

In region W2, herons, kestrels and barn owls tended to contain low DDE residues, yet sparrowhawks contained very high residues. Sample location maps of DDE residues in the trauma and the remainder groups for sparrowhawks are shown in Figure 25, and, for comparison, kestrels (Figure 26). For the total sample of kestrels, the geometric mean residue of DDE was significantly higher in region E4 than in W2 (t_{107}=3.26, P<0.01), but, for the sparrowhawk liver samples, the mean residue level in region W2 was slightly higher than in region E4.

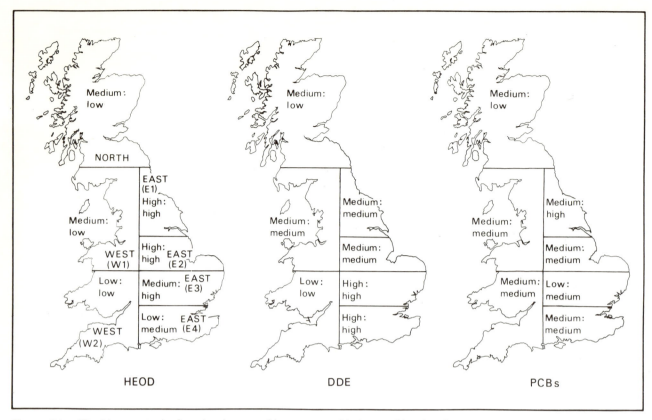

Figure 24. 'Residue status' of regional areas. Liver organochlorine residue levels; trauma:all samples.

Unlike the situation for HEOD and DDE, no region stood out as having consistently high mean residues of PCBs (Table 15); no clear regional differences were apparent. For sparrowhawks, kestrels and barn owls, however, mean residues in the North region tended to be low. The distribution of residues is shown for kestrels (Figure 27), the species for which most data were available. No 'hot spots' for PCBs were apparent.

iii. Numbers of samples exceeding particular levels in different regions: As very few samples had residues in excess of 100 ppm DDE or PCBs, numbers of samples with residues exceeding 10 ppm DDE or PCBs were also recorded. This exercise permits an assessment of the geographical distribution of samples with these comparatively high residue loads. In general, such geographical trends as were observed

TABLE 13

Examination of samples by regions: geometric mean of HEOD residues for trauma group and for total samples of each species.

		Heron			Sparrowhawk			Kestrel			Barn owl
Region	*n*	Geometric mean (ppm) (range of values within 1 standard error)	*n*	Geometric mean (ppm) (range of values within 1 standard error)		*n*	Geometric mean (ppm) (range of values within 1 standard error)		*n*	Geometric mean (ppm) (range of values within 1 standard error)	
Trauma											
W1	6	0.49 (0.28–0.86)	22	0.21 (0.13–0.35)		13	0.57 (0.45–0.71)		15	0.11 (0.06–0.19)	
W2	5	0.03 (0.01–0.10)	24	0.54 (0.37–0.77)		13	0.51 (0.36–0.72)		13	0.31 (0.18–0.50)	
E1	0		2	5.29 (2.00–14.0)		8	0.86 (0.65–1.13)		5	2.10 (1.30–3.41)	
E2	11	0.35 (0.14–0.86)	2	0.42 (0.20–0.90)		11	2.16 (1.24–3.75)		30	0.92 (0.75–1.13)	
E3	19	0.36 (0.22–0.61)	5	0.40 (0.13–1.26)		23	0.70 (0.47–1.04)		36	0.84 (0.69–1.02)	
E4	14	0.19 (0.09–0.41)	16	0.46 (0.28–0.75)		24	0.32 (0.22–0.45)		21	0.44 (0.36–0.56)	
N	5	0.44 (0.27–0.70)	17	0.17 (0.10–0.30)		8	0.57 (0.39–0.84)		3	0.95 (0.30–3.01)	
Total											
W1	16	0.65 (0.44–0.97)	36	0.42 (0.29–0.61)		40	0.75 (0.64–0.89)		36	0.60 (0.41–0.89)	
W2	16	0.60 (0.29–1.22)	52	0.46 (0.34–0.62)		38	0.45 (0.34–0.60)		23	0.48 (0.35–0.66)	
E1	0		7	5.01 (2.66–9.43)		34	1.82 (1.42–2.33)		18	3.52 (2.51–4.95)	
E2	23	0.77 (0.42–1.41)	7	3.10 (1.63–5.90)		41	3.23 (2.49–4.18)		49	1.53 (1.21–1.92)	
E3	47	1.43 (1.01–2.05)	9	0.66 (0.30–1.49)		109	2.23 (1.83–2.72)		75	1.64 (1.37–1.97)	
E4	28	0.87 (0.53–1.42)	36	0.52 (0.38–0.73)		71	0.56 (0.45–0.69)		44	1.01 (0.81–1.27)	
N	13	0.42 (0.28–0.65)	36	0.32 (0.21–0.49)		29	1.04 (0.74–1.45)		6	1.29 (0.71–2.33)	

TABLE 14

Examination of samples by regions: geometric mean of DDE residues for trauma group and for total samples of each species.

Region		Heron Geometric mean (ppm) (range of values within 1 standard error)		Sparrowhawk Geometric mean (ppm) (range of values within 1 standard error)		Kestrel Geometric mean (ppm) (range of values within 1 standard error)		Barn owl Geometric mean (ppm) (range of values within 1 standard error)
	n		n		n		n	
Trauma								
W1	6	7.97 (3.07–20.7)	22	2.17 (1.61–2.93)	13	0.80 (0.44–1.46)	15	0.09 (0.05–0.14)
W2	5	0.57 (0.30–1.06)	24	5.38 (4.17–6.94)	13	0.66 (0.48–0.91)	13	0.07 (0.03–0.17)
E1	0		2	2.83 (2.00–4.00)	8	0.68 (0.37–1.24)	5	0.56 (0.16–1.96)
E2	11	1.80 (1.11–2.90)	2	2.86 (2.00–4.10)	11	1.17 (0.68–1.99)	30	0.44 (0.30–0.65)
E3	19	1.89 (1.36–2.62)	5	5.28 (3.38–8.25)	23	1.06 (0.79–1.42)	36	0.67 (0.52–0.86)
E4	14	3.60 (2.01–6.45)	16	3.04 (1.58–5.87)	22	1.67 (1.21–2.31)	21	0.31 (0.19–0.49)
N	5	2.91 (1.39–6.11)	17	2.17 (1.42–3.32)	8	1.16 (0.75–1.79)	3	1.14 (0.32–4.03)
Total								
W1	16	4.81 (2.86–8.08)	36	3.38 (2.58–4.43)	40	1.18 (0.87–1.59)	36	0.63 (0.42–0.95)
W2	16	3.09 (1.88–5.08)	52	7.11 (5.66–8.93)	38	0.89 (0.65–1.22)	23	0.16 (0.10–0.28)
E1	0		7	5.41 (2.98–9.80)	34	0.76 (0.54–1.08)	18	1.06 (0.62–1.82)
E2	23	3.57 (2.50–5.10)	7	4.14 (2.50–6.84)	41	1.97 (1.45–2.68)	49	0.51 (0.34–0.76)
E3	47	6.63 (5.00–8.79)	9	6.59 (4.27–10.2)	109	1.83 (1.45–2.32)	75	1.01 (0.78–1.31)
E4	28	8.32 (5.83–11.9)	36	6.52 (4.54–9.39)	71	2.78 (2.56–3.43)	44	1.07 (0.70–1.65)
N	12	3.72 (2.18–6.35)	36	2.02 (1.41–2.89)	30	1.12 (0.82–1.53)	6	0.45 (0.22–0.93)

TABLE 15

Examination of samples by regions: geometric mean of PCB residues for trauma group and for total samples of each species.

Region		Heron Geometric mean (ppm) (range of values within 1 standard error)		Sparrowhawk Geometric mean (ppm) (range of values within 1 standard error)		Kestrel Geometric mean (ppm) (range of values within 1 standard error)		Barn owl Geometric mean (ppm) (range of values within 1 standard error)
	n		n		n		n	
Trauma								
W1	6	5.65 (2.99–10.7)	17	1.59 (1.02–2.42)	10	1.13 (0.45–2.84)	11	0.07 (0.04–0.14)
W2	4	1.67 (0.93–3.00)	18	2.07 (1.39–3.09)	8	0.96 (0.44–2.12)	11	0.11 (0.05–0.27)
E1	0		2	4.00 (4.00–4.00)	4	0.03 (0.01–0.10)	2	3.55 (3.00–4.20)
E2	10	2.47 (1.34–4.55)	2	5.11 (3.00–8.70)	9	0.78 (0.41–1.47)	25	0.08 (0.05–0.13)
E3	18	2.11 (1.11–4.01)	4	1.75 (0.99–3.02)	20	0.28 (0.15–9.53)	31	0.09 (0.05–0.14)
E4	11	2.37 (1.14–4.90)	12	1.24 (0.58–2.67)	15	1.47 (0.91–2.38)	15	0.21 (0.10–0.42)
N	3	4.95 (2.00–12.2)	16	1.11 (0.62–1.99)	5	0.40 (0.15–1.03)	2	0.10 (0.01–1.00)
Total								
W1	14	3.61 (1.66–7.86)	27	2.05 (1.37–3.05)	23	2.15 (1.34–3.42)	27	0.61 (0.34–1.09)
W2	13	3.29 (1.75–6.19)	39	3.11 (2.28–4.24)	22	0.89 (0.54–1.30)	15	0.12 (0.06–0.24)
E1	0		6	3.14 (1.82–5.43)	20	0.76 (0.42–1.38)	8	2.47 (1.05–5.78)
E2	14	6.09 (3.24–11.5)	5	5.04 (2.95–8.62)	34	0.89 (0.59–1.32)	41	0.12 (0.08–0.19)
E3	44	7.41 (5.21–10.5)	8	2.43 (1.42–4.17)	93	0.76 (0.58–1.00)	60	0.18 (0.13–0.26)
E4	19	4.86 (2.93–8.06)	28	2.42 (1.55–3.76)	53	1.90 (1.49–2.41)	31	0.55 (0.34–0.89)
N	11	6.21 (3.75–10.3)	32	0.96 (0.60–1.51)	19	0.30 (0.17–0.53)	5	0.03 (0.01–0.06)

were in agreement with those noted above for mean residue levels (Table 16). For HEOD, most of the high-residue samples came from regions E1, E2 and E3, in which 104 samples out of 419 (25%) had residues of 10 ppm or more HEOD, compared with only 33 samples out of 521 (6%) from elsewhere; the difference was highly significant ($\chi^2 = 63.6$, $P < 0.001$).

In the East region, high residues of DDE became relatively more common from north to south. Region E4 had the greatest percentage of residues exceeding both the 10 ppm and 100 ppm limits. Geographical differences were not as marked as they were for HEOD residues.

Again for PCBs, there were no marked regional trends. Region W1 had the highest percentage of samples with levels of 10 ppm or more (32%), but even there only one sample had PCB residues in excess of 100 ppm.

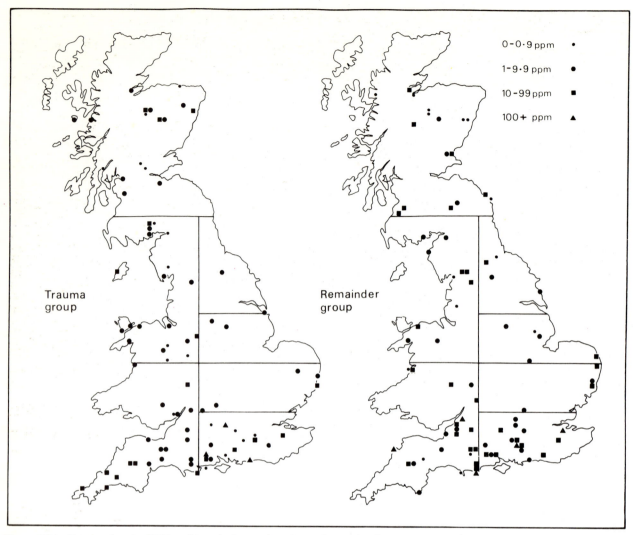

Figure 25.   Sparrowhawk: DDE residues in livers; locations of samples from trauma and remainder groups.   The regional areas are shown.

iv. Discussion: HEOD frequently showed geographical variations, with high residues in birds from areas where wheat suffers seriously from bulb fly. Bell (1975) drew attention to the high residue concentration among kestrels and barn owls collected from 1970 to 1973 inside the wheat bulb fly areas. From the material presented here for trauma and remainder samples collected over a much longer time period, it seems that kestrels display such geographical variations to a much greater degree than barn owls, despite the fact that barn owls are believed to be more sedentary. Although herons were unlikely to have derived significant HEOD residues from seed dressings, they also tended to have high residues in the wheat bulb fly areas. These residues may have originated from run-off from farmland, from other agricultural uses in the intensively-agricultural east of England or perhaps from industrial sources (see Prestt 1970).

When regions were defined as in Figure 24, it was found that mean levels tended to be highest in regions E1, E2 and E3. That birds in E2 and E3 were heavily contaminated was not surprising. Taken together, these regions corresponded fairly closely with the East Midlands and East Region of MAFF, in which aldrin and dieldrin usage is known to have been the highest for England and Wales (Cook 1964). Scientists at PICL have studied wildlife casualties involving agricultural chemicals for many years. During the period 1967-1972, out of 49 incidents in England and Wales that were attributed to dieldrin poisoning, 36 (74%) were reported from regions E2 and E3, as defined in this report (Bunyan & Stanley 1973). Relatively few samples from region E1 were received at Monks Wood, but these samples tended to contain similar concentrations of HEOD to samples from regions E2 and E3.

It is interesting to reflect on the geographical distribution of carcases sent to Monks Wood. Taking into account the distribution of breeding birds (Sharrock 1976), a disproportionately large number of herons, kestrels and barn owls came from the wheat bulb fly area of eastern England. This was even true of the trauma groups (eg see barn owl, Figure 23). Monks Wood Experimental Station is situated within the wheat bulb fly area and possibly this encouraged local interest, but barn owls killed by trauma and sent to MAFF at Tolworth in Surrey had a comparable distribution of origin (Stanley & Elliott 1976).

Plate 5.   *Female heron with large nestlings. A fish-eater, this is the main species used in our programme to monitor pollution in lakes and rivers.*
Photo: A. A. Bell.

Plate 6.   *Thin-shelled heron eggs broken and ejected by the parents. Shell-thinning is caused by DDE, the main metabolite of the insecticide DDT.*
Photo: A. A. Bell.

Plate 7. *Great crested grebe (above), and kingfisher (below): fish-eaters which are also vulnerable to the presticides and pollutants which enter our rivers and lakes.*
Grebe photo: R. T. Smith. Kingfisher photo: R. K. Murton.

Plate 8.   Golden eagle at nest. When dieldrin was used widely in sheep dips, the breeding success of this species declined in western Scotland where eagles often take sheep carrion as food.
Photo: R. T. Smith.

Plate 9.   Sparrowhawk, one of the species most affected by organochlorine pesticides, and one of the main species used in our pesticide monitoring programme.
Photo: R. T. Smith.

Plate 10. (Top left) Merlin with prey. Feeding on small birds, this species suffered marked declines in numbers and breeding success during the main period of organochlorine use in the early 1960s. It breeds on moorlands but moves to lower agricultural and coastal areas for the winter.
Photo: R. T. Smith.

Plate 11. (Top right) Kestrel at nest hole. Breeding commonly throughout Britain and feeding mainly on small rodents, this species has proved to be a good subject for the long-term monitoring of pesticide residues.
Photo: R. K. Murton.

Plate 12. (Bottom left) Tawny owl, a woodland species which feeds mainly on small rodents and accumulates pesticide residues, but usually not in sufficient amounts to affect its numbers and breeding.
Photo: R. T. Smith.

Plate 13. Barn owl with young at nest. A rodent-eater, mainly on farmland, this species is vulnerable to pesticides, and was used in our monitoring programme.
Photo: R. T. Smith.

Plate 14. Long-eared owl (left) and little owl (right). These species also accumulate organochlorine pesticides, but it is not certain whether their numbers and breeding success have been affected.
Photos: R. T. Smith.

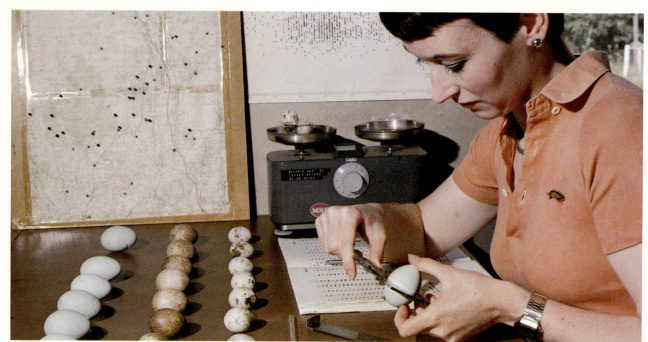

Plate 15. *Measuring the thickness of heron, peregrine and sparrowhawk egg shells.*
Photo: I. Wyllie

Plate 16. *A normal clutch of sparrowhawk eggs.*
Photo: I. Newton.

Plate 17. *Thin-shelled sparrowhawk eggs, found broken in the nest. The thinning is caused by DDE, the main metabolite of the insecticide DDT.*
Photo: I. Newton

The geographical distribution of DDE residues in these avian samples was markedly different from that of HEOD. The highest DDE residues were found in region E4, which was apparently relatively unpolluted with HEOD. Region E3 contained samples that tended to be rather less heavily polluted with DDE and a north-south trend was noted in DDE residues in the eastern half of England. In the past, when birds were poisoned in the field by DDT, it was thought to have been due to its use in orchards. Thus, out of 41 incidents that were attributed to DDT by PICL during the period 1964-1975, 38 (93%) were in orchards (Anon 1978). Typically, the species killed were songbirds, such as blackbirds and song thrushes, but it is possible that, when high levels of DDE were found in the livers of birds of prey and herons, they may have originated from orchard uses of DDT. Certainly the most extensive areas of orchards are in south-east England (Coppock 1964) coinciding with region E4. In 1958, the county of Kent contained 33% of the whole area of England and Wales under 'top' fruit (apples, pears, plums, etc). Moving north up the eastern side of England, fruit-growing becomes progressively less important. The north-south trend in the extent of fruit-growing areas fits the relative magnitude of DDE

residues to be found in predatory birds. Important fruit-growing localities also occur in the south-west in region W2. This is the only fruit-growing region in which sparrowhawks were comparatively common (see Prestt 1965), and here sparrowhawks tended to be very heavily contaminated with DDE. Data for the other species studied did not, however, reflect this trend.

It would be unrealistic to ascribe all high levels of DDE in bird tissues to DDT use in orchards. In the early 1960s, DDT was used on a similar area of other crops (principally wheat, brassicas and peas) as on top fruit (Cook 1964), and it is still used for some purposes today. Uses on other crops also lead to residues in wildlife samples. Invertebrates accumulate residues and these might be taken by ground-feeding birds, which in turn could be eaten by predators. Earthworms and other invertebrates at arable sites were found by Davis (1968) to contain measurable amounts of DDE and related compounds, but the concentrations were considered to be insufficient to cause acute poisoning in birds taking such organisms. In 1976, staff of PICL noticed a change in the pattern of poisoning incidents involving DDT (Anon 1978). During the first four

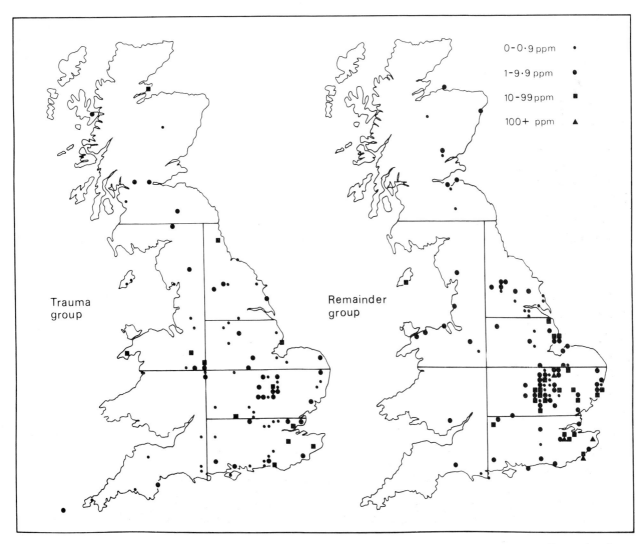

Figure 26. Kestrel: DDE residues in livers; locations of samples from trauma and remainder groups. The regional areas are shown.

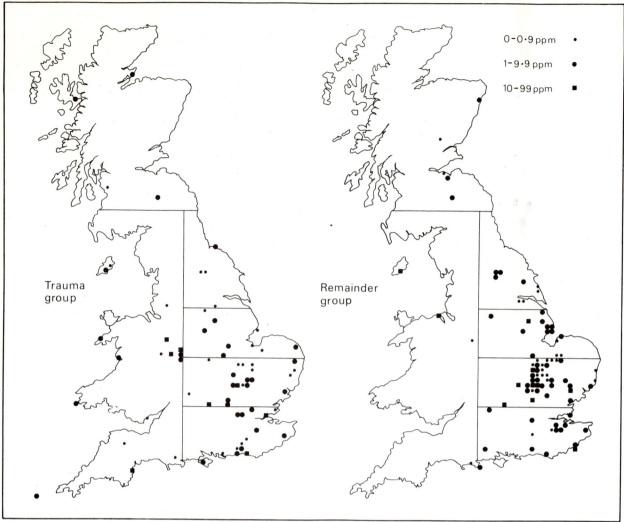

Figure 27.   Kestrel: PCB residues in livers; locations of samples from trauma and remainder groups.   The regional areas are shown.

months of the year, a series of 15 incidents was described involving mainly redwings *(Turdus iliacus)*, long-eared owls and kestrels. These were believed to be birds that had just migrated to Britain from the continent. It was suggested that residues had been acquired on the continent (or perhaps by the kestrels in Britain during the previous year), had been mobilised as the fat supplies were depleted during migration, and had ultimately proved lethal. Many of these incidents occurred in Kent, which is nearer to the European mainland than the rest of Britain, and all but one were reported from south-east England or East Anglia. Therefore high residues of DDE in birds in region E4 should not necessarily be blamed on local orchard use of DDT. It is conceivable that, even before 1976, a significant amount of this pollution was of 'foreign' origin. Sedentary British birds of prey might also acquire appreciable residues of DDE by feeding on immigrant prey-species, which were themselves highly contaminated.

With respect to PCB residues, there were no clear regional trends. This finding is in agreement with the observations of Prestt *et al.* (1970). They reported on the residues in the samples sent to Monks Wood in the period 1966-1968 and concluded that, for the terrestrial environment, "It would appear that PCB is available in all regions of Britain and its distribution appears to be random rather than by area".

Organochlorine residues in other species

Six other species were collected and analysed throughout the period 1963-1977. Of these 50-100 livers of two species were analysed, the great crested grebe and kingfisher, while fewer analyses were made on other species (golden eagle, rough-legged buzzard, peregrine and long-eared owl). Material for the grebe and kingfisher was treated separately, and more fully than data for the remaining species. Data for an additional six species analysed from 1963-1966 are presented later (p.49).

Great crested grebes and kingfishers

For great crested grebes and kingfishers (Plate 7), there were sufficient analyses to determine whether seasonal, annual and regional trends were in general agreement with those in other species. The main interest was comparison with the heron, the other fish-eating species feeding mainly in the fresh-water environment.

TABLE 16

Examination of samples by regions: percentage of samples with residue levels of 10 ppm or more or 100 ppm or more.

Region	W1 %≥10	W1 %≥100	W2 %≥10	W2 %≥100	E1 %≥10	E1 %≥100	E2 %≥10	E2 %≥100	E3 %≥10	E3 %≥100	E4 %≥10	E4 %≥100	N %≥10	N %≥100
HEOD														
Heron	6	0	6	0	0	0	22	0	23	0	7	0	0	0
Sparrowhawk	3	0	0	0	57	0	29	0	11	0	3	0	8	0
Kestrel	5	0	5	0	21	0	37	0	30	0	7	0	17	0
Barn owl	11	0	4	0	28	0	16	0	17	0	11	0	0	0
ALL 4 SPECIES	6	0	3	0	27	0	25	0	24	0	7	0	9	0
DDE														
Heron	31	6	31	0	0	0	35	0	49	9	61	7	33	8
Sparrowhawk	25	0	46	6	29	0	14	0	33	0	47	14	28	0
Kestrel	10	0	5	0	6	0	15	0	23	2	23	6	13	0
Barn owl	11	0	4	0	11	0	12	2	12	0	18	5	0	0
ALL 4 SPECIES	17	1	25	2	10	0	18	1	25	3	32	7	21	1
PCBs														
Heron	57	7	38	0	0	0	43	14	52	7	47	0	36	0
Sparrowhawk	30	0	28	0	17	0	20	0	13	0	32	0	22	0
Kestrel	26	0	9	0	15	5	6	0	14	0	15	0	0	0
Barn owl	26	0	0	0	38	0	2	0	5	0	13	0	0	0
ALL 4 SPECIES	32	1	20	0	21	3	11	2	20	1	23	0	16	0

TABLE 17

Geometric mean residues in the livers of great crested grebes and kingfishers, 1963-1977.

		Trauma group Geometric mean (ppm) (range of values within 1 standard error)		Total samples Geometric mean (ppm) (range of values within 1 standard error)
	n		n (%≥10,%≥100)	
HEOD				
Great crested grebe	30	0.04 (0.03–0.07)	52 (0,0)	0.08 (0.05–0.12)
Kingfisher	22	0.83 (0.65–1.05)	63 (11,0)	1.51 (1.27–1.80)
DDE				
Great crested grebe	30	1.72 (1.27–2.33)	51 (41,0)	2.22 (1.66–2.96)
Kingfisher	22	1.94 (1.44–2.60)	63 (35,2)	3.86 (3.17–4.69)
PCBs				
Great crested grebe	24	2.77 (1.78–4.30)	41 (59,10)	5.30 (3.47–8.08)
Kingfisher	22	1.05 (0.60–1.84)	56 (39,0)	2.14 (1.52–2.99)

Great crested grebes contained very low HEOD residues, while kingfishers had relatively high concentrations, higher even than those in kestrels and barn owls (Tables 4 & 17). Although the level of HEOD tended to be higher in kingfishers than in herons, the proportion of samples with residues of 10 or more ppm was only 11% in kingfishers compared with 14% in herons. Like herons, kingfishers contained comparatively high concentrations of DDE, but concentrations in grebes were slightly lower on average. Great crested grebes had very high concentrations of PCBs, similar to those in herons. Ten percent of the grebes contained at least 100 ppm PCBs. Kingfishers contained rather lower PCB residues, but still had more in their livers than sparrowhawks, kestrels or barn owls. The poor-condition group of grebes had especially high residues: geometric mean concentrations were 7.7 ppm DDE (n=11) and 58.5 ppm PCBs (n=9).

The figures for the three aquatic species suggest that there has been substantial pollution of the freshwater environment in Britain by DDE and PCBs. The situation as regards HEOD is less clear, as kingfishers and herons contained substantial quantities, but grebes had very low concentrations. This may be due at least partly to habitat differences between the species (see Prestt & Jefferies 1969), kingfishers and herons favouring flowing water, such as streams, drainage channels and rivers, and grebes favouring isolated water bodies, such as gravel pits and reservoirs. Perhaps the former environment in Britain has been much more polluted with HEOD than the latter.

i. Seasonal variations. To give reasonable sample sizes, carcases were assigned to periods of three months and means calculated (Table 18). For great crested grebes, residues of DDE and PCBs were

TABLE 18

Geometric mean residues in the livers of great crested grebes and kingfishers during each three-month period.

Months	n	HEOD Geometric mean (ppm) (range of values within 1 standard error)	n	DDE Geometric mean (ppm) (range of values within 1 standard error)	n	PCBs Geometric mean (ppm) (range of values within 1 standard error)
Great crested grebe						
Jan.-Mar.	15	0.08 (0.03–0.18)	14	1.30 (0.73–2.31)	9	2.71 (1.00–7.31)
Apr.-Jun.	25	0.07 (0.04–0.12)	25	3.55 (2.60–4.83)	21	8.90 (5.64–14.0)
Jul.-Sept.	10	0.12 (0.05–0.30)	10	3.13 (1.91–5.12)	9	8.19 (4.61–14.6)
Oct.-Dec.	12	0.02 (0.01–0.05)	12	2.64 (1.15–6.08)	10	3.17 (1.05–9.52)
Kingfisher						
Jan.-Mar.	19	2.15 (1.64–2.81)	19	5.46 (3.90–7.64)	17	5.68 (3.41–9.47)
Apr.-Jun.	16	1.53 (1.01–2.31)	16	5.53 (3.40–8.99)	13	1.73 (0.69–4.37)
Jul.-Sep.	15	0.94 (0.65–1.36)	15	2.77 (1.80–4.26)	14	1.11 (0.57–2.17)
Oct.-Dec.	14	1.69 (1.15–2.47)	14	2.86 (2.06–3.96)	13	1.82 (1.04–3.19)

highest during the second quarter of the year, but only slightly lower in the third quarter. This trend was rather different from those noticed previously in herons, sparrowhawks, kestrels and barn owls, for which autumn residues were generally very low. HEOD residues for grebes were too low to be able to conclude with confidence whether any seasonal trend existed. Kingfishers conformed more closely to the usual pattern, with highest residues in the first and second quarters of the year.

ii. Variations in residue levels, 1963-1977: Analytical data were grouped into the same time periods used for the 4 main species and mean residues calculated (Table 19). For great crested grebes, there were no marked changes in DDE or PCB content over the years. The absence of a drop in PCB residues in 1977 was in contrast to the trend shown by herons (Table 10), though samples were few. Residues in kingfishers showed similar changes to those in herons, but unfortunately no residue figures were available for 1977. Both kingfishers and herons

showed a progressive decrease in mean HEOD levels between periods. Residues of DDE in kingfishers fell steadily during the period under review, while for herons they fell from a peak in the late 1960s (Table 9). PCB residues showed no change from 1966-1971 to 1972-1975.

This material lends further support to the idea that great crested grebes have been exposed to different sources of residues than those confronting kingfishers and herons.

iii. Geographical variations: No carcases were available from the north region for either species. In order to produce reasonable sample sizes, some amalgamation of sub-regions was necessary. This was done in accordance with regional trends in residue levels observed for the four principal species, and in such a way as to determine whether similar trends existed for grebes and kingfishers. Mean residues are shown in Table 20.

TABLE 19

Geometric mean residues in the livers of great crested grebes and kingfishers for the periods indicated.

Period	n	HEOD Geometric mean (ppm) (range of values within 1 standard error)	n	DDE Geometric mean (ppm) (range of values within 1 standard error)	n	PCBs Geometric mean (ppm) (range of values within 1 standard error)
Great crested grebe						
1963-1965	13	0.06 (0.02–0.14)	13	3.33 (2.23–4.97)	0	
1966-1971	24	0.05 (0.03–0.09)	24	3.85 (2.71–5.47)	23	7.08 (4.42–11.4)
1972-1975	21	0.14 (0.08–0.23)	20	1.28 (0.72–2.26)	21	4.84 (2.49–9.39)
1977	4	0.01 (0.00–0.03)	4	5.09 (2.63–9.87)	4	6.65 (2.56–17.2)
Kingfisher						
1964-1965	4	6.83 (3.95–11.8)	4	7.43 (5.69–9.70)	0	
1966-1971	37	1.56*(1.24–1.98)	37	4.35 (3.26–5.82)	34	1.97 (1.28–3.02)
1972-1975	22	1.16 (0.89–1.53)	22	2.86 (2.09–3.90)	22	2.52 (1.43–4.46)
1977	0		0		0	

*significantly different from mean of previous period, P<0.05.

TABLE 20

Geometric mean residues in the livers of great crested grebes and kingfishers for the regions indicated.

Regions		Great crested grebe			Kingfisher	
	n	Geometric mean (ppm) (range of values within 1 standard error)		n	Geometric mean (ppm) (range of values within 1 standard error)	
HEOD						
W1+W2	18	0.02	(0.01–0.04)	10	2.21	(1.24–3.94)
E1+E2+E3	30	0.05	(0.03–0.09)	36	1.78	(1.43–2.21)
E4	9	0.39**	(0.17–0.87)	18	1.01	(0.74–1.38)
DDE						
W1+W2	18	0.96	(0.55–1.69)	10	3.79	(2.50–5.74)
E1+E2	14	2.22	(1.45–3.40)	11	10.8	(7.71–15.1)
E3+E4	24	6.42**	(4.61–8.94)	43	3.21	(2.48–4.15)
PCBs						
W1+W2	15	2.28	(1.14–4.54)	7	1.91	(0.98–3.70)
E1+E2	13	3.44	(1.57–7.55)	10	7.53	(4.66–12.2)
E3+E4	17	16.8*	(10.2–27.6)	40	1.71	(1.10–2.66)

Significantly different from mean of W1+W2, *, $P<0.05$; **, $P<0.01$.

Neither species contained particularly high HEOD levels in the area E1+E2+E3. Since cyclodiene usage has probably been most intense in this area, it seems that seed dressings were not the main source of the HEOD acquired by grebes and kingfishers. The tendency for herons to have high residues in this area (Table 13) was not as marked as it was for, say, kestrels.

Great crested grebes had highest DDE residues in the south-east corner of England (E3+E4). Herons showed the same trend (Table 14,) but kingfishers were most contaminated in the north-east (E1+E2). PCB residues displayed parallel trends to DDE residues in grebes and kingfishers.

iv. Discussion: Even in the most recent years of the survey, great crested grebes were still contaminated with DDE and PCBs, especially in the south-east corner of England. They contained very little HEOD, possibly because they usually frequent those types of enclosed isolated waters that have remained relatively free from HEOD pollution. Kingfishers, on the other hand, have evidently been very polluted with all three residues. Concentrations of HEOD and DDE have tended to fall since the early 1960s. These patterns of contamination are similar to those shown by herons. Although both kingfishers and herons tend to feed on fish from flowing water, they differ in the spatial patterns of contamination. In kingfishers, the sources of high residues of HEOD in the west and of DDE in the north-east remain to be defined. Relatively high residues of DDE in great crested grebes after mid-summer have also been noted by Lukowski (1978).

Golden eagles (Plate 8), ***rough-legged buzzards, peregrines*** (Cover) ***and long-eared owls*** (Plate 14) ***1963-1977.***
Analytical data for these species are treated briefly, because few carcases were received and several papers have already been published on them (eg Jefferies & Prestt 1966; Prestt et al. 1968; Lockie & Ratcliffe 1964; Lockie et al. 1969; Ratcliffe, 1972, 1973; Prestt & Ratcliffe 1972; Anon 1978).

Peregrine livers were especially polluted with all three residues; long-eared owls contained high levels of HEOD and DDE, while rough-legged buzzards were particularly contaminated with HEOD (Table 21). A substantial proportion of the carcases of these three species had liver concentrations of HEOD or DDE or PCBs sufficiently high to suggest death by poisoning. The following percentages of carcases had liver residues of 10 ppm or more HEOD, of 100 ppm or more DDE, of 100 ppm or more PCBs: rough-legged buzzard, 63%; peregrine, 20%; long-eared owl, 33%. In contrast, none of the 10 golden eagles contained more than 6 ppm of any pollutant residue in the liver and mean residue levels were generally very low, especially of HEOD and PCBs.

Common buzzards (Buteo buteo) (Plate 19), ***hen harriers*** (Circus cyaneus), ***merlins*** (Falco columbarius) (Plate 10), ***little owls*** (Athene noctual) (Plate 14), ***tawny owls*** (Strix aluco) (Plate 12) ***and short-eared owls*** (Asio flammeus), ***1963-1966.***
Samples from these species were analysed during the period 1963-1966 only (Table 22), after which analysis was discontinued for all except the merlin because residues were considered to be low. The merlin was

TABLE 21

Geometric mean residues in the livers of golden eagles, rough-legged buzzards, peregrines and long-eared owls.

		Trauma group		Total samples	
	n	Geometric mean (ppm) (range of values within 1 standard error)	*n*(%≥10,%≥100)		Geometric mean (ppm) (range of values within 1 standard error)
HEOD					
Golden eagle	4	0.07 (0.02–0.31)	9 (0,0)		0.02 (0.01–0.07)
Rough-legged buzzard	0		8 (63,0)		2.35 (0.61–9.05)
Peregrine	5	1.99 (1.15–3.46)	15 (7,0)		1.91 (1.35–2.71)
Long-eared owl	13	0.78 (0.38–1.59)	30 (30,0)		1.75 (1.14–2.70)
DDE					
Golden eagle	4	0.27 (0.06–4.49)	10 (0,0)		0.21 (0.10–0.45)
Rough-legged buzzard	0		8 (0,0)		0.05 (0.02–0.16)
Peregrine	5	9.20 (3.85–22.0)	15 (47,0)		7.56 (4.81–11.9)
Long-eared owl	13	2.64 (1.77–3.96)	29 (45,7)		5.97 (4.28–8.33)
PCBs					
Golden eagle	1	0.0	4 (0,0)		0.0
Rough-legged buzzard	1	1.0	5 (0,0)		0.17 (0.05–0.57)
Peregrine	4	23.0 (10.6–50.1)	10 (50,20)		9.37 (3.93–22.3)
Long-eared owl	10	0.15 (0.07–0.33)	21 (10,0)		0.38 (0.22–0.67)

excluded from the present scheme after 1966 because it was another bird-feeder like the sparrowhawk and peregrine (which were being studied in some depth) and few carcases were being received.

The few merlin samples that were available were highly contaminated. Of the five livers analysed, four contained more than 20 ppm DDE. That merlins are at risk from pesticides has been appreciated by conservationists; Newton (1973) concluded: "Though breeding on remote moorlands, the merlin moves to lowland areas for the winter, and is there exposed to contamination by pesticides. An examination of the BTO nest record cards reveals a similar pattern of breeding failure to that reported for the peregrine and sparrowhawk in recent years. Losses of part and even whole clutches after the start of incubation, combined with egg-breakage, egg-shell thinning, and the presence of residues in the eggs, show that this small falcon is gravely at risk." Later findings in Northumberland (Newton *et al.* 1978) were consistent with organochlorine-induced breeding failures having occurred in this species in the 1960s, but the incidence of failure was reduced in the 1970s.

The mean residues observed in the samples of these species are compared with those in other species below (Table 23).

Organochlorine residues in tissues: some general conclusions

Over the years, many comprehensive reviews have appeared on this subject (eg Moore 1965; Robinson 1967, 1969; Mellanby 1967; Prestt & Ratcliffe 1972; Moriarty 1975; Newton 1979) and there is little point in repeating what these authors have said. Here, discus-

sion is limited to a few topics that either represent new ideas, or are worth reconsidering now that more data are available.

Following the pioneering work of Moore and Walker (1964), it has often been stated that birds with the highest residues are terrestrial predators feeding on other birds, or aquatic predators feeding on fish. This generalisation has been borne out by the substantial amount of analytical material presented here. Chemical analyses have been performed on 10 species since 1963 and on another six species during the mid-1960s. Species are tabulated according to the mean residue level for total samples (Tables 23-25). Principal types of food are also given; why certain species were assigned particular principal dietary components requires a little explanation. Rough-legged buzzards are normally regarded as predators of mammals, at least where they breed (Brown 1976). This species has, however, been observed to feed on dead wood-pigeons during the winter in Britain and acquire lethal residues of HEOD (Prestt *et al.* 1968). Therefore here their food is given as mammals and birds. The rough-legged buzzards analysed were all found dead in eastern England. The preferred food of long-eared owls is similarly classified. Generally, this species eats more rodents than birds (Everett 1977), but the long-eared owls on which autopsies have been performed at Monks Wood have often contained remains of passerines in their gizzards, especially greenfinches *(Carduelis chloris)*. Song birds are believed to be taken from roosts. The greenfinch was one of the species most commonly found dead in poisoning incidents on agricultural land in the late 1950s and early 1960s (eg see Cramp *et al.* 1962). The diet of the golden eagle is classified as 'mammals' because, apart from the lagomorphs and deer carrion that eagles are known to

Plate 18. Barn owl: one of the species which declined, particularly in south-east England, during the peak period of aldrin/dieldrin use.
Photo: R. T. Smith.

Plate 19. *Buzzards at nest. Feeding on birds and mammals, and breeding mainly in northern and western districts, this species accumulates pesticide residues, but usually not sufficiently to affect its breeding success or numbers. Photo: R. T. Smith.*

TABLE 22

Geometric mean residues in the livers of common buzzards, hen harriers, merlins, little owls, tawny owls and short-eared owls.

	n	Trauma group Geometric mean (ppm) (range of values within 1 standard error)		n	Total samples Geometric mean (ppm) (range of values within 1 standard error)	
HEOD						
Common buzzard	4	1.08	(0.54–2.16)	12	0.62	(0.35–1.10)
Hen harrier	0			8	0.17	(0.06–0.52)
Merlin	2	2.12	(0.90–5.00)	5	1.31	(0.77–2.23)
Little owl	10	0.02	(0.01–0.04)	20	0.03	(0.02–0.06)
Tawny owl	28	0.09	(0.06–0.14)	55	0.15	(0.11–0.20)
Short-eared owl	2	0.04	(0.01–0.30)	6	0.08	(0.02–0.28)
DDE						
Common buzzard	4	0.10	(0.02–0.53)	12	0.06	(0.03–0.15)
Hen harrier	0			8	1.54	(0.96–2.45)
Merlin	2	34.9	(27.0–45.0)	5	21.1	(12.9–35.1)
Little owl	10	0.33	(0.14–0.76)	20	0.76	(0.46–1.26)
Tawny owl	28	0.63	(0.44–0.91)	55	1.06	(0.77–1.46)
Short-eared owl	2	0.2	(in both)	6	1.72	(0.76–3.88)

take, their organochlorine residues are believed to have come from eating sheep carrion, after the sheep had been dipped (Lockie *et al.* 1969).

In the table for HEOD (Table 23), the order of contamination seems independent of diet. There is no reason to suppose that mammal-feeders would contain differing amounts than other species, since those feeding on rodents in agricultural situations will have been exposed to HEOD used as seed dressings. Thus, kestrels and barn owls are quite high in the list. As noted previously, the three species that feed primarily on fish differed greatly in mean HEOD concentration. Species differences of this type may be due at least partly to physiological and metabolic differences, and not only to variations in exposure via the diet. Whatever the mechanism, however, there are marked differences in the DDE and PCB levels that seem to confirm earlier statements about relationships with diet. For DDE (Table 24), the species down to and

including great crested grebe all feed on birds or fish to an appreciable extent. For species below the grebe, mammals figure prominently in the diet. The same is true for PCBs (Table 25), the division in this case occurring between sparrowhawk and kestrel; the mean residue for the sparrowhawk was twice that for the kestrel.

At this juncture, it is interesting to examine the liver residue levels in the various species in the light of recent population trends in Britain. Of the ten species analysed into the 1970s, only one, the rough-legged buzzard, does not breed here. Of the remaining nine, sparrowhawk, peregrine, kestrel and barn owl have suffered population declines believed to be associated with mortality induced by HEOD, and the first two have also experienced breeding failure supposedly caused by HEOD, DDE (DDT) and perhaps PCBs (eg see Prestt 1965; Prestt & Ratcliffe 1972; Ratcliffe 1972, 1973; Newton & Bogan 1978). Golden eagles,

TABLE 23

Species analysed in the scheme, arranged in order of mean liver residues of HEOD in all samples.

	Period covered	Mean HEOD in liver (ppm)	Principal dietary components
Rough-legged buzzard	1966–1976	2.35	mammals/birds
Peregrine	1963–1975	1.91	birds
Long-eared owl	1964–1977	1.75	mammals/birds
Kingfisher	1964–1976	1.51	fish
Merlin	1964–1966	1.31	birds
Barn owl	1963–1975	1.21	mammals
Kestrel	1963–1975	1.20	mammals
Heron	1963–1975	0.87	fish
Common buzzard	1963–1966	0.62	mammals
Sparrowhawk	1963–1975	0.50	birds
Hen harrier	1963–1966	0.17	mammals
Tawny owl	1963–1965	0.15	mammals/birds
Great crested grebe	1963–1977	0.08	fish
Short-eared owl	1963–1965	0.08	mammals
Little owl	1963–1965	0.03	invertebrates/mammals/birds
Golden eagle	1963–1973	0.02	mammals

TABLE 24

Species analysed in the scheme, arranged in order of mean liver residues of DDE in all samples.

	Period covered	Mean DDE in liver (ppm)	Principal dietary components
Merlin	1964–1966	21.1	birds
Peregrine	1963–1974	7.56	birds
Long-eared owl	1964–1977	5.97	mammals/birds
Heron	1963–1975	5.29	fish
Sparrowhawk	1963–1975	4.42	birds
Kingfisher	1964–1976	3.86	fish
Great crested grebe	1963–1977	2.22	fish
Short-eared owl	1963–1965	1.72	mammals
Kestrel	1963–1975	1.59	mammals
Hen harrier	1963–1966	1.54	mammals
Tawny owl	1963–1965	1.05	mammals/birds
Little owl	1963–1965	0.76	invertebrates/mammals/birds
Barn owl	1963–1975	0.70	mammals
Golden eagle	1963–1973	0.21	mammals
Common buzzard	1963–1966	0.06	mammals
Rough-legged buzzard	1966–1976	0.05	mammals/birds

TABLE 25

Species analysed in the scheme, arranged in order of mean liver residues of PCBs for all samples.*

	Period covered	Mean PCBs in liver (ppm)	Principal dietary components
Peregrine	1969–1974	9.37	birds
Heron	1967–1975	5.55	fish
Great crested grebe	1968–1977	5.30	fish
Kingfisher	1967–1976	2.14	fish
Sparrowhawk	1967–1975	2.02	birds
Kestrel	1967–1975	1.01	mammals
Long-eared owl	1968–1977	0.38	mammals/birds
Barn owl	1967–1975	0.24	mammals
Rough-legged buzzard	1967–1976	0.17	mammals/birds
Golden eagle	1968–1973	0.0	mammals

*PCBs were not analysed until 1967, so there are fewer species in this table than in tables 23-24.

although containing very low residues in this survey, are considered to have suffered reproductive failure in the western highlands of Scotland because of HEOD contamination (Lockie *et al.* 1969; but see also p.67). Long-eared owls have suffered widespread declines over England and Wales, the reasons for which have not been clearly defined, but pesticides do not appear to have been implicated (Parslow 1973). This leaves the three species that feed mainly on fish: heron, great crested grebe and kingfisher. Generally, they have had high liver residues of organochlorines, but none is thought to have declined markedly as a consequence, although the heron, at least, has suffered reproductive failure because of these pollutants (Prestt 1970; Cooke *et al.* 1976). Populations of these fish-eating species have fared remarkably well considering their high residues. One possible explanation is that they escaped the lethal effect of HEOD because their intake of this chemical was chronic rather than acute (see discussion in Prestt 1970). Organisms may have a greater tolerance to chronic doses of an organochlorine than to massive acute doses that result in similar body or tissue concentra-

tions (eg Cooke 1973b). Mortality by HEOD was probably the single most significant factor in causing the marked population declines of several raptor species in Britain (Prestt 1965; Jefferies & Prestt 1966; Young 1968; Ratcliffe 1970; Cooke 1973a). Heron populations may also be able to withstand breeding failure better than raptors because of the ability of herons to lay repeat clutches (see Prestt 1970; Cooke *et al.* 1976).

This report confirms the conclusions of previous authors (eg Mellanby 1967; Robinson 1967; Prestt & Ratcliffe 1972), that a relatively small proportion of carcases of most species contained enough organochlorine to make one suspect poisoning as the cause of death (Table 4). However, this study did not begin until after the major population declines of predatory birds had occurred (eg see Prestt 1965), and followed a marked decline in residues in dead birds noted at the beginning of the 1960s (Robinson 1967). Many more of the dead birds examined had liver residues that could be indicative of harmful, sublethal effects. The proportion of individuals with high residues was consistently smaller for the trauma group than for total carcase samples.

Marked seasonal changes in liver residues were noted, together with regional variations that were reasonably consistent between species. Seasonal changes appeared to be related more to physiological changes in body composition than to environmental availability of pollutants. In the East region, during the first six months of the year, the percentage of carcases with residues of at least 10 ppm HEOD was consistently higher for each species than in the whole of Britain, viewed throughout the year (Table 26). It is in the east of England that species suffered most severely from organochlorines. Here, the sparrow-hawk virtually disappeared, kestrels and barn owls decreased appreciably and herons suffered reproductive failure (Prestt 1965, 1970). Any recovery in population by birds of prey will have been impeded by an apparently considerable loss of birds to poisoning by HEOD. Thus, 37% of all the kestrels picked up dead in the East during the first six months of the year from 1963 to 1975 had liver levels of HEOD indicative of death by poisoning. If one is still more selective, for regions E1, E2 and E3, during the months of January, February and March, 58% of the dead kestrels contained at least 10 ppm HEOD. The birds with high residues of HEOD in the liver were usually birds of reasonable body weight, and a considerable proportion of potential breeding birds must have been removed from these raptor populations in eastern England just before, or during, the breeding season. In addition, DDE and PCBs have probably caused some deaths, and to these must be added the sublethal effects induced by all the organochlorines. It is therefore not surprising that the sparrowhawk is only very slowly

TABLE 26

Percentage of liver samples with at least 10 ppm HEOD, 1963–1975. Number of samples analysed is given in brackets.

		Trauma group	Total
Heron	Britain, all year	5% (60)	14% (143)
	East, all year	7% (44)	18% (98)
	Britain, January–June	9% (34)	21% (97)
	East, January–June	13% (24)	27% (67)
Sparrowhawk	Britain, all year	1% (93)	7% (195)
	East, all year	4% (25)	14% (59)
	Britain, January–June	2% (52)	9% (116)
	East, January–June	7% (15)	17% (35)
Kestrel	Britain, all year	5% (101)	18% (374)
	East, all year	6% (64)	24% (255)
	Britain, January–June	11% (46)	33% (183)
	East, January–June	14% (29)	37% (128)
Barn owl	Britain, all year	3% (123)	14% (251)
	East, all year	3% (92)	17% (186)
	Britain, January–June	6% (72)	22% (155)
	East, January–June	6% (51)	25% (114)

returning to this area (Sharrock 1976; Cooke et al. 1979).

The first of the restrictions on organochlorine insecticide usage was a voluntary ban from 1961 on using cyclodiene seed dressings in the spring. This ban appears to have been beneficial to wildlife, as the widespread incidents involving grain-eating birds became much less common and residues in tissues had decreased by 1962/1963 (Robinson 1967). Robinson also noted that there was no further decline in residue concentrations up to 1965. It was immediately after this initial decline in residue levels that the present scheme was started. In herons, kingfishers and sparrowhawks, residues of HEOD showed some decrease in the 1960s, as there were further restrictions on the uses of cyclodienes, but in other species HEOD levels were still very high in the early 1970s. By 1977, residues had decreased markedly in all species. At the end of 1975, there had been a final ban on the use of cyclodienes as seed dressings, but residues in kestrels and barn owls had started to fall before this date. These conclusions are supported by information from the PICL 'incidents' scheme involving agricultural chemicals. It should, however, be pointed out that livers from a few birds collected in 1978 and 1979 did contain 10 or more ppm HEOD.

The impact of the restrictions in cyclodiene usage on the six principal species may be summarised as follows: the kestrel and barn owl, because of their feeding habits, only showed a decrease in residues towards the end of the period during which cyclodiene seed dressings were phased out. The sparrowhawk was already very rare in the cereal-growing areas when the survey began, but the few carcases from the east frequently contained high residues of HEOD. Residues generally decreased in the late 1960s following restrictions. If the survey had been started before 1961, massive residues of HEOD may well have been recorded regularly in sparrowhawks found dead in the east of England. HEOD residues declined rapidly in the kingfisher in the 1960s, and decreased steadily in the heron from the late 1960s. The great crested grebe does not appear to have been exposed to appreciable amounts of HEOD.

Some species (such as the heron, barn owl, kingfisher) showed a decline in DDE residues with time, but others (sparrowhawk, kestrel, great crested grebe) did not, and levels in 1977 were similar to those in 1963-65. For several species, there was a peak in residue levels in the late 1960s. Some of this DDE may have been of foreign origin. PICL reported a series of incidents in 1976 involving immigrant birds that died in Britain from DDE poisoning, presumably after mobilising stored residues during migration (Anon 1978). Kestrels were amongst the birds concerned, and in 1976, DDE reached a massive peak in the livers of birds analysed in the present scheme. Here again there was agreement between the two schemes.

Liver residues of PCBs have shown significant declines in kestrels, barn owls and herons, but only in kestrels did the decline coincide with the ban introduced by Monsanto in 1971. Residues in sparrowhawks and great crested grebes have remained high.

Some of the changes in residue levels recorded over the years may have been due to sampling bias, with high proportions of samples in some years originating during the spring, when residues tended to be high. In fact, any effect of seasonal bias could be discounted. Since all three organochlorine residues tended to reach their peak at about the same time of year, any bias resulting from a high proportion of spring birds should have caused an increase in all residues, but trends in annual mean levels tended to differ between HEOD, DDE and PCBs. In years when high mean residues were recorded, consideration was also given to the possibility that this was due to a high proportion of samples being collected from the most contaminated (eastern) regions. However, an increase in the proportion of carcases from a contaminated region may have been the result of increased pollution in that particular year. Examining data for the kestrel, the years in which the highest percentages of samples were received from the most contaminated regions (E1+E2+E3) were 1970 (69%) and 1973 (77%). Mean HEOD residues were high in kestrel livers in 1970 (1.33 ppm) and especially so in 1973 (2.92 ppm). However, referring to information from the PICL 'incident scheme', it is evident that unusually high percentages of incidents were caused by dieldrin in 1970 and 1973. There is thus no evidence to link the increase in mean DDE residues noted during the late 1960s with sampling bias alone.

In the USA, a National Pesticide Monitoring Program was started in 1964. This is a combined study by several federal agencies to monitor organochlorines in water, soil, air, food, plants, animals and people. As regards residues in wildlife, O'Shea and Ludke (1979) concluded: ''Although such facts point out the all-pervasive nature of contamination with organochlorine chemicals, the monitoring of trends through time leads to a cautiously optimistic outlook. Concentrations of DDT and DDE, for example, have generally decreased in freshwater fish, starlings and ducks during the 1970's. This is an encouraging sign that reflects the 1972 ban imposed on the general use of DDT in the United States. Optimism must remain guarded, however: residues of some pollutants have failed to decline in fish and birds despite restrictions on their use. Although key industries have voluntarily restricted their use of PCB's and regulations have been instituted that limit PCB discharges into the Nation's lakes and streams, concentrations of these chemicals in fish and wildlife tissues have not yet shown consistent declines.'' The situation in the USA appears to be broadly similar to that in Britain.

Mercury concentrations in herons, sparrowhawks, kestrels and barn owls

Total mercury concentrations in liver samples were ascertained as ppm dry weight. Preliminary statistical analysis showed no significant differences in levels between the sexes or the age classes.

Concentrations in different species and different categories of death

Only 10 heron livers were analysed, but they contained significantly higher mercury concentrations than livers of sparrowhawks ($t_{77}=6.87$, $P<0.001$), which in turn contained higher concentrations than livers of barn owls ($t_{189}=3.86$, $P<0.001$), which in turn contained slightly more mercury than livers of kestrels ($0.05<P<0.1$) (Table 27). These differences may be 'natural' due to variations in the physiology or ecology of the species concerned rather than to interspecific variations in exposure to mercury pollution. Osborn (1978) and Osborn et al. (1979) found mercury levels in the livers of some breeding seabirds that were similar to those found in herons.

At present the significance of these mercury concentrations is not known, but if agricultural mercury had made any significant contribution to the residues, high levels might have been expected in kestrels and barn owls, which were likely to take small mammals that had fed on grain treated with organomercurial fungicides (Jefferies et al. 1973; Stanley & Elliott 1976; Anon 1978). In fact, these two species contained less mercury than the herons and sparrowhawks.

TABLE 27

Geometric mean concentrations of mercury in the livers of herons, sparrowhawks, kestrels and barn owls, 1968–1976.

		Heron			Sparrowhawk			Kestrel			Barn owl	
	n	Geometric mean (ppm) (range of values within 1 standard error)		n	Geometric mean (ppm) (range of values within 1 standard error)		n	Geometric mean (ppm) (range of values within 1 standard error)		n	Geometric mean (ppm) (range of values within 1 standard error)	
Trauma	5	24.4	(16.5–36.2)	38	5.67	(5.23–6.16)	51	3.89	(3.61–4.19)	76	4.00	(3.81–4.21)
Poor-condition	2	37.4	(31.1–45.0)	4	6.47	(4.74–8.84)	42	4.71	(4.43–5.02)	21	5.44**	(4.80–6.16)
Remainder	3	21.6	(17.5–26.6)	27	7.71*	(6.78–8.75)	57	4.01	(3.74–4.30)	25	6.70***	(6.01–7.46)
TOTAL SAMPLES	10	25.6	(20.9–31.5)	69	6.44	(6.01–6.92)	150	4.15	(3.99–4.33)	122	4.69	(4.47–4.92)

Significantly different from mean of trauma group, *, $P<0.05$; **, $P<0.01$; ***, $P<0.001$.

Mercury concentrations differed considerably from organochlorine concentrations in that ranges and standard errors were relatively much smaller. Stanley and Elliott (1976) made the same observation. There was also little difference (except in barn owls) between the mean for the trauma group and the means for the other groups (Table 27).

Stanley and Elliott analysed the livers of barn owls killed by trauma and found an arithmetic mean (±S.E.) of only 1.16±0.26 ppm dry weight (n=9), ie 3-4 times lower than the geometric mean found for the trauma group in the present survey. This discrepancy has no obvious explanation, but the sample size was rather small.

Variations in mercury levels during the year

Bell et al. (1978) have already presented graphs showing monthly mean residue levels for total samples of sparrowhawks and barn owls. They made the following comments: "Both the kestrel and barn owl exhibit a peak in liver mercury residues in December, the source of the mercury presumably being the autumn cereal dressings accumulated via the small rodent prey which both these species eat. In the kestrel, mercury residues decline during the spring months to reach their lowest level in May, in spite of the fact that most spring barley is planted in March and early April and is dressed with mercury compounds. A proportion of birds then show high liver residues in June. In contrast, in the barn owl, mercury residues start to rise during the spring, so that peak residues are found in May, a trend consistent with contamination from the spring sowings. It is extremely difficult to account for these species' differences on ecological grounds and it is likely that they reflect physiological differences." The graphs showed a peak around May and/or June for each species, but sample sizes were very small in these months, varying from two to seven.

Compared with the changes through the year for liver residues of organochlorines, the variation from month to month in mercury concentration was relatively slight. Furthermore, there was no consistent overall pattern for changes in mercury levels between the three species, in contrast to the spring peak almost invariably shown by organochlorine residues. Non-parametric statistical tests on seasonal trends have shown that significant differences exist between mercury concentrations in different months, eg in kestrels levels were significantly lower in May than in December ($U_{4,7}=0$, $P<0.05$).

In other birds, metal levels are known to vary through the year, in association with the changes in body condition that accompany breeding and moult. In starlings, liver mercury concentrations are very low during the summer moult, but rise later in the year when the birds turn to newly-sown winter wheat and ingest the associated organomercurial fungicides

(Osborn 1979). In waders, increased concentrations of zinc, mercury and cadmium occur in livers prior to pre-nuptial moult (Ward & Evans in preparation). Possible relationships have been considered between metal concentration and moult in the kestrel (moult begins at the end of May), sparrowhawk (early May for female, June for male) and barn owl (April): mean mercury concentrations rose in them all at the onset of moult and fell again rapidly. Changes in zinc content were similar. In the late autumn, mercury in the livers of kestrels and barn owls increased again, as it did in starlings (Osborn 1979). It should be stressed again, however, that the work on predators was done on old material and sample sizes were very small, especially in the summer months, so further work is required to check these trends.

Variations in mercury levels from year to year

Storage, freezing and thawing the samples may have led to loss of mercury, so to find whether any significant change in time had occurred, the main period for analysis was divided in half, results for 1970-1972 being tested against those for 1973-1975 (Table 28). In fact the older samples generally had rather higher mercury concentrations, significantly more in the case of kestrel and barn owl. The reason for this is not clear, as no bans have been imposed on the use of mercury compounds in Britain. Stanley and Elliott (1976) detected no significant change in mercury in barn owl tissue during the period 1967-1973. In the Netherlands and Sweden, where restrictions were imposed on the use of alkyl mercury as a seed dressing, decreases in mercury levels in birds of prey followed (Borg et al. 1969; Ackefors 1971; Fuchs et al. 1971; Stanley & Elliott 1976). Conceivably, the decrease in mercury concentration noted in dead kestrels in Britain was due partly to migrant individuals acquiring lower levels on the continent. However, the restrictions in the Netherlands and Sweden were in the 1960s and led to immediate decreases in mercury concentrations in those countries, whereas the decreases in Britain appear to have occurred rather later, in the 1970s.

Geographical variations in mercury levels

Mean concentrations of mercury in livers from each region are given in Table 29. Regional 'scores' and 'residue status' were calculated for the three species involved in the same way as for organochlorines (Figure 28). Residues tended to be slightly higher in regions E2 and E3, the main cereal-growing areas of England. Mean levels in region E3 were significantly higher throughout than those in regions E1 or N (Mann-Whitney $U_{6,6}=0$, $P<0.05$). Differences between means for any pairs or groups of samples were, however, small and non-significant.

There was some tendency for barn owls with the highest concentrations to be found in the east where

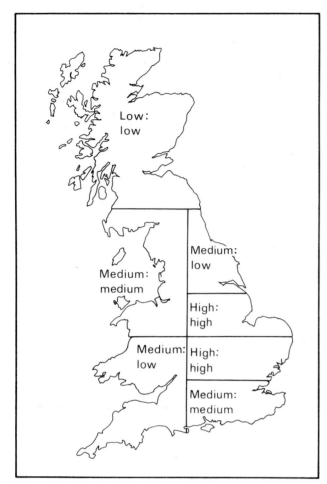

Figure 28. Regional 'residue status'. Liver mercury levels; trauma: all samples.

most of our cereals are grown and mercury usage in agriculture is presumably greatest (Figure 29). Eleven of the 13 livers with more than 9 ppm of mercury came from the East region. However, the proportion of birds with high concentrations (>6 ppm) in the East, or in the area of wheat bulb fly attack, was not significantly different from the proportion found in the rest of Britain.

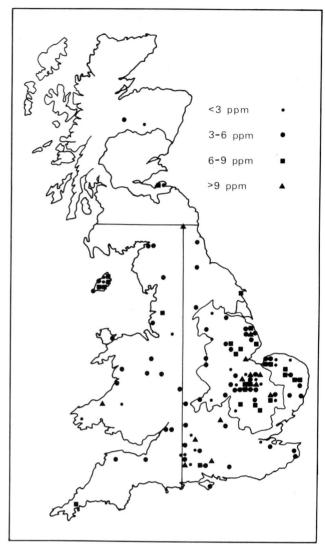

Figure 29. Barn owl, 1968-1976: liver mercury levels. North, east and west regions are shown, as are the two main areas of wheat bulb fly attack.

Concentrations in the Isle of Man tended to be unusually high (Figure 29). It may be significant that Parslow and Jefferies (1975) found that mercury

TABLE 28

Geometric mean concentrations of mercury in the livers of sparrowhawks, kestrels and barn owls in different periods.

		Sparrowhawk		Kestrel		Barn owl
	n	Geometric mean (ppm) (range of values within 1 standard error)	n	Geometric mean (ppm) (range of values within 1 standard error	n	Geometric mean (ppm) (range of values within 1 standard error)
Trauma						
1970–72	5	5.59 (3.73–8.39)	13	6.08 (4.98–7.43)	24	4.55 (4.08–5.08)
		$t_4 = 0.103$		$t_{14} = 2.970$ D*		$t_{34} = 1.389$
1973–75	30	5.36 (4.96–5.79)	34	3.28 (3.11–3.47)	49	3.85 (3.65–4.05)
Total						
1970–72	13	5.82 (4.87–6.94)	36	5.72 (5.14–6.38)	48	5.48 (5.08–5.90)
		$t_{62} = 0.008$		$t_{43} = 3.729$ D***		$t_{117} = 2.414$ D*
1973–75	51	5.80 (5.39–6.24)	110	3.74 (3.60–3.88)	71	4.35 (4.10–4.62)

t-test: significantly different, *, P<0.05; ***, P<0.001. D=decrease.
    degrees of freedom were calculated using the formula given in Bailey (1959) for the comparison of means of two samples where the variances were unequal.

TABLE 29

Examination of samples by regions: geometric mean of mercury residues for trauma group and for total samples for each species.

Region		Sparrowhawk		Kestrel		Barn owl
	n	Geometric mean (ppm) (range of values within 1 standard error)	n	Geometric mean (ppm) (range of values within 1 standard error)	n	Geometric mean (ppm) (range of values within 1 standard error)
Trauma						
W1	12	6.40 (5.62–7.30)	8	3.73 (3.02–4.62)	10	3.79 (3.52–4.08)
W2	12	5.17 (4.43–6.02)	8	4.30 (3.57–5.16)	8	3.54 (3.24–3.87)
E1	1	5.74	6	3.80 (3.37–4.29)	1	2.55
E2	0		4	3.78 (3.37–4.23)	20	4.21 (3.81–4.65)
E3	2	5.93 (3.98–8.83)	12	4.25 (3.30–5.47)	24	4.10 (3.75–4.49)
E4	5	5.70 (4.93–6.60)	9	3.50 (3.35–3.65)	11	4.17 (3.40–5.12)
N	6	5.27 (3.87–7.18)	4	3.61 (2.91–4.48)	2	3.87 (3.69–4.06)
Total						
W1	17	6.80 (6.03–7.67)	17	4.06 (3.54–4.65)	18	4.36 (4.00–4.76)
W2	21	6.76 (5.92–7.73)	15	4.73 (4.16–5.37)	12	4.14 (3.66–4.70)
E1	4	6.49 (5.27–8.00)	13	4.73 (3.44–4.05)	5	4.24 (3.49–5.15)
E2	0		20	4.25 (3.81–4.73)	29	5.04 (4.58–5.54)
E3	4	9.37 (6.80–12.9)	44	4.30 (3.89–4.74)	35	4.98 (4.50–5.49)
E4	11	5.15 (4.59–5.81)	31	3.92 (3.70–4.14)	19	4.63 (3.97–5.40)
N	12	5.94 (4.69–7.51)	10	4.03 (3.50–4.56)	4	4.02 (3.40–4.77)

residues in guillemot eggs were highest in colonies around the Irish Sea. They remarked that "this is . . . presumably connected with the slow rate of water exchange in the relatively shallow Irish Sea as well as the larger amounts of industrial waste and effluent it receives". The terrestrial environment of the Isle of Man, situated as it is in the centre of the Irish Sea, also seems to be relatively rich in mercury.

Organochlorine residues in bird eggs

During the 1960s and 1970s, the eggs of several species were collected and analysed, including more than 100 eggs for each of the following species: grey heron, golden eagle, sparrowhawk and peregrine (Plates 15, 16 & 17). Much has been published already on the residues found in the eggs of these four species (eg see Lockie et al. 1969; Prestt 1970; Ratcliffe 1970; Prestt & Ratcliffe 1972; Newton & Bogan 1974, 1978; Cooke et al. 1976), so we shall concern ourselves here with the changes in residues over the years. Results from the eggs of other species are not included as these were given by Ratcliffe (1970) and Prestt and Ratcliffe (1972).

Materials and methods

Collection of heron eggs was fairly systematic. Fresh eggs were taken from nests at five heronries, mainly in 1966, 1968, 1970, 1973 and 1977 (Plates 20, 21 & 22). Residues in eggs collected up to 1973 were discussed by Prestt (1970) and Cooke et al. (1976). In 1977, several eggs were taken from the Troy colony and one egg from Willoughby (both heronries are in Lincolnshire). Only from Troy were eggs obtained in each of the five years. Collection of eggs from nests of golden eagles, sparrowhawks and peregrines was necessarily opportunistic, and hence less systematic.

For each species, geometric mean residue levels in each year were calculated to determine trends with time. Eggs were also assigned to regions to study regional variations. Specimens were analysed by gas-liquid chromatography, mostly in the Laboratory of the Government Chemist. Residues were expressed as ppm wet weight.

Results and observations

Grey heron eggs
Residues in eggs from the Troy heronry are shown in Figure 30. Only one egg per clutch was included because within-clutch variation was very small (Prestt 1970). Mean HEOD levels decreased significantly from 1966 to 1968 ($P<0.01$) and from 1968 to 1970 ($P<0.01$). Mean DDE levels also decreased steadily from 1966 to 1973, the change from 1966 to 1968 being statistically significant ($P<0.05$). Neither HEOD nor DDE showed appreciable changes from 1970 to 1977. Mean PCB concentrations tended to rise after 1970, and the difference between 1970 and 1977 was significant ($P<0.01$).

A greater proportion of eggs had PCB residues of 10 ppm or more after 1970, and in 1977, two eggs

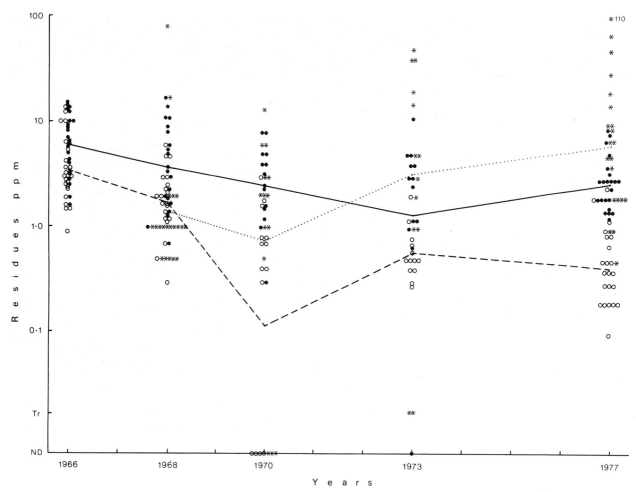

*Figure 30. Heron eggs, Troy colony: ○, HEOD; ●, DDE; *, PCBs. Residues for the main years of collection. Geometric means: ― ― ― ―, HEOD; —————, DDE; ·········, PCBs.*

contained more than 100 ppm PCBs (Figure 31). This tendency was restricted to eggs from Troy; the combined sample of eggs collected from the other four heronries did not show this trend (Figure 32), although sample sizes were small after 1968. Mean residues in eggs collected from these other colonies were tabulated by Cooke *et al.* (1976).

For most of the heron eggs, the month of laying was known. Mean concentrations of each of the three organochlorines increased during the laying period, March-May (Table 30). This trend was not due to collection being biased towards certain months in certain years.

Golden eagle eggs

Material used here includes that presented by Lockie *et al.* (1969), plus more recent results. Few eagle eggs contained detectable amounts of PCBs, and only HEOD and DDE levels are presented. Egg residues of HEOD and DDE showed similar trends, declining rapidly during the second half of the 1960s (Figure 33).

Lockie *et al.* (1969) and Ratcliffe (1970) separated eggs from western Scotland and the Islands from eggs laid in the central and eastern Highlands on the basis of organochlorine levels, those from the west being higher. The decreases in HEOD and DDE residues for the total sample were due to significant decreases in residues in eggs collected from the west (Table 31).

TABLE 30

Geometric mean residues in heron eggs collected from colonies in eastern England during the months of March, April and May (1964–1977).

	n	HEOD Geometric mean (ppm) (range of values within 1 standard error)	n	DDE Geometric mean (ppm) (range of values within 1 standard error)	n	PCBs Geometric mean (ppm) (range of values within 1 standard error)
March	135	0.75 (0.65–0.86)	135	2.52 (2.23–2.85)	96	1.11 (0.90–1.38)
April	103	1.19* (1.05–1.35)	103	4.68***(4.25–5.14)	74	1.98 (1.56–2.53)
May	45	3.20***(2.64–3.88)	45	5.55 (4.92–6.26)	16	7.02[a] (32.8–15.0)

t-test: significantly different from previous month, *, P<0.05; ***, P<0.001.
significantly different from March, [a], P<0.05.

Plate 20. Heron on nest. Although accumulating relatively high organochlorine residue levels, population numbers have remained remarkably constant.
Photo: R. K. Murton.

Plate 21. Checking heron nest contents with a mirror.
Photo: I. Wyllie.

Plate 22. Collecting a sample of heron's eggs for chemical analysis. The nests in this colony range in height between 45 and 60 feet.
Photo: I. Wyllie.

Plate 23. Sparrowhawk at nest. This species almost disappeared from eastern districts during the peak period of aldrin/dieldrin use, and declined elsewhere.
Photo: R. K. Murton.

Plate 24. Peregrine at nest. This species suffered a marked population decline during the peak period of aldrin/dieldrin use, and virtually disappeared from the south and east coasts of England.
Photo: R. T. Smith.

TABLE 31

Geometric mean residues in golden eagle eggs.

		Western Scotland			East & Central Scotland			Total samples	
	n	Geometric mean (ppm) (range of values within 1 standard error)		*n*	Geometric mean (ppm) (range of values within 1 standard error)		*n*	Geometric mean (ppm) (range of values within 1 standard error)	
HEOD									
1964–65	37	0.45	(0.37–0.56)	1	Trace		38	0.40	(0.32–0.51)
1966–71	38	0.09***	(0.07–0.12)	14	0.03	(0.02–0.04)	52	0.07***	(0.05–0.09)
1972–74	7	0.03	(0.01–0.09)	3	0.01	(0.00–0.05)	10	0.03	(0.01–0.05)
ALL EGGS	82	0.17	(0.14–0.21)	18	0.02[aaa]	(0.02–0.03)	100	0.12	(0.10–0.15)
DDE									
1964–65	37	0.29	(0.22–0.39)	1	Trace		38	0.26	(0.20–0.36)
1966–71	38	0.14**	(0.11–0.17)	14	0.03	(0.02–0.04)	52	0.09**	(0.07–0.11)
1972–74	7	0.15	(0.08–0.29)	3	0.09	(0.04–0.19)	10	0.13	(0.08–0.21)
ALL EGGS	82	0.19	(0.16–0.23)	18	0.03[aa]	(0.02–0.04)	100	0.14	(0.12–0.17)

t-test: significantly different from previous period, **, $P<0.01$; ***, $P<0.001$.
significantly different from west, [aa], $P<0.01$; [aaa], $P<0.001$.

Sparrowhawk eggs

In the total sample, mean DDE residues declined during the late 1960s and early 1970s, whereas PCBs increased during this period (Figure 34). HEOD residues tended to be low during 1968-1970. Only one egg was analysed after 1972.

Eggs were assigned to one of the three regions: (1) the east (as in Figure 24) excluding the New Forest, (2) the north and west, and (3) the New Forest. Eggs from the New Forest were treated separately because they

Figure 31. Heron eggs, Troy colony: number of eggs (one per clutch) with residues of different magnitude.

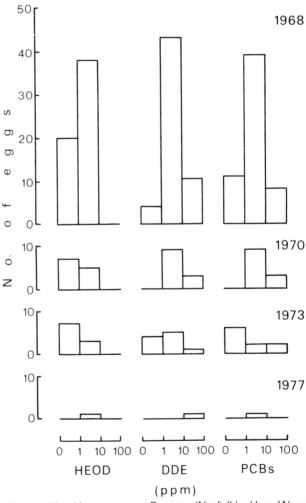

Figure 32. Heron eggs, Denver (Norfolk), Hag Wood, Newball and Willoughby (all Lincolnshire) colonies: number of eggs (one per clutch) with residues of different magnitude.

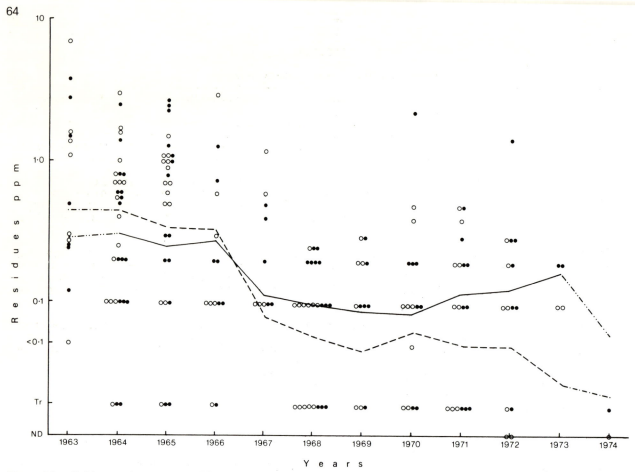

Figure 33. Golden eagle eggs: ○, HEOD; ●, DDE. Residues (one egg per clutch) year by year. 3-yearly trend in geometric means· — — — —, HEOD (— · — · — ·, where 2-year values only available); —————, DDE (—··—··—).

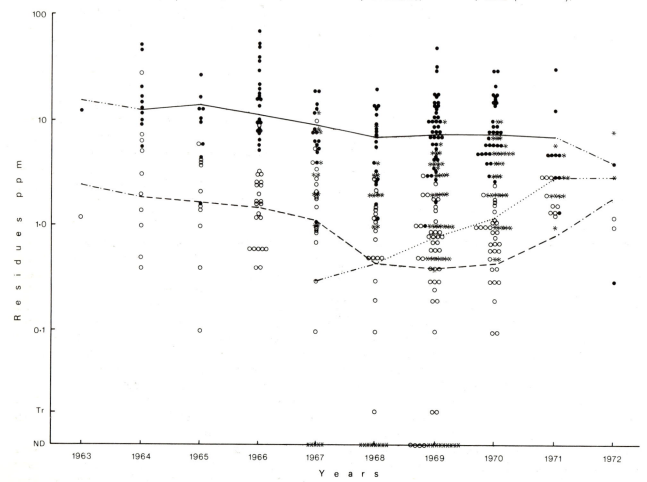

Figure 34. Sparrowhawk eggs: ○, HEOD; ●, DDE; *, PCBs. Residues (one egg per clutch) year by year. 3-yearly trend in geometric means: — — — —, HEOD (— · — · — · —, where 2-year values only available); —————, DDE (—··—··—); ·······, PCBs (—···—·).

TABLE 32

Geometric mean residues in sparrowhawk eggs.

		East			New Forest			North and West			Total samples	
		Geometric mean (ppm) (range of values within			Geometric mean (ppm) (range of values within			Geometric mean (ppm) (range of values within			Geometric mean (ppm) (range of values within	
	n	1 standard error)		n	1 standard error)		n	1 standard error)		n	1 standard error)	
HEOD												
1963–65	7	4.92	(3.97–6.09)	7	0.88	(0.66–1.18)	10	2.09	(1.34–3.28)	24	2.09	(1.63–2.67)
1966–71	22	1.71*	(1.36–2.14)	19	0.56	(0.48–0.66)	113	0.60*	(0.51–0.71)	154	0.69**	(0.60–0.79)
1972	0			0			2	1.10	(1.0–1.2)	2	1.10	(1.0–1.2)
ALL EGGS	29	2.02^a	(1.81–2.69)	26	0.63	(0.55–0.73)	125	0.67	(0.57–0.79)	180	0.81	(0.71–0.91)
DDE												
1963–65	7	16.6	(15.7–17.6)	7	12.2	(9.50–15.6)	10	10.1	(7.26–14.1)	24	12.3	(10.5–14.4)
1966–71	22	11.9	(9.80–14.6)	19	14.2	(12.1–16.7)	113	7.20	(6.74–7.69)	154	8.41*	(7.90–8.96)
1972	0			0			2	1.10	(0.3–0.4)	2	1.10	(0.3–4.0)
ALL EGGS	29	12.9	(11.1–15.1)	26	14.1	(12.3–16.1)	125	7.18^b	(6.69–7.70)	180	8.69	(8.16–9.24)
PCBs												
1967–71	17	2.18	(1.49–3.20)	10	2.49	(1.33–4.66)	102	0.63	(0.50–0.79)	129	0.82	(0.67–1.01)
1972	0			0			2	4.90	(3.0–8.0)	2	4.90	(3.0–8.0)
ALL EGGS	17	2.18	(1.49–3.20)	10	2.49	(1.33–4.66)	104	0.65^c	(0.52–0.82)	131	0.85	(0.69–1.03)

t-test: significantly different from previous period, *, $P<0.05$; **, $P<0.01$.
significantly different from New Forest or North and West, ^{a}, $P<0.001$.
significantly different from East or New Forest, ^{b}, $P<0.001$.
significantly different from East, ^{c}, $P<0.05$.

were fairly numerous and showed rather different trends in residue levels from elsewhere. Egg residues of HEOD decreased significantly in the east and in the north and west from 1963-1965 to 1966-1971 (Table 32). HEOD residues were highest in the east, while DDE residues were highest in the east and in the New Forest. Although there was an overall decrease in DDE residues from 1963-1965 to 1966-1971, those in the New Forest tended to increase. During 1966-1971, DDE residues in eggs from the New Forest were significantly higher than residues in eggs from the north and west ($P<0.001$). Residues of PCBs were highest in eggs collected in the east and the New Forest.

Peregrine eggs

In the overall sample, DDE residues tended to decline from the early 1960s to the early 1970s (Figure 35). Mean HEOD residues decreased from about 1965 to 1967. Residues of PCBs were variable, tending to be highest in 1972 and 1977.

The regional division of Ratcliffe (1970) and Prestt and Ratcliffe (1972) was adopted, and eggs from the east and central Highlands were compared with those from the rest of Britain (Table 33). The mean level of HEOD decreased significantly in the 'rest' of Britain from 1963-1965 to 1966-1971; overall, HEOD levels were lower in the east and central Highlands of Scotland than elsewhere. Mean DDE levels decreased in both regions in the 1960s and early 1970s; DDE levels were lower in samples from the east and central Highlands. During the 1970s, PCBs tended to increase in the 'rest' of Britain. Like HEOD and DDE, levels of PCBs were lower in the east and central Highlands than elsewhere (Plate 24).

Discussion

In all four species, egg residues of HEOD and DDE decreased considerably during the latter part of the 1960s. Reductions in HEOD content may have been due to the restrictions imposed. The ban on the use of dieldrin in sheep dips was introduced in 1966, and 1967 marked the start of the decline in annual mean HEOD residues in eggs of the eagle, the only species of those considered that was exposed to HEOD in sheep carrion (Lockie et al. 1969). However, mean DDE in eagle eggs also began to decrease in 1967 and there was a marked similarity in the three-year trends for both residues (Figure 33). Less information was available on changes in PCB levels, but there was evidently a local increase in heron eggs collected at the Troy colony in the 1970s (Figure 30), and there were signs of increases in sparrowhawk and peregrine eggs at the same time (Figures 34 and 35).

Only in sparrowhawks and herons were both eggs and livers examined. HEOD residues in the livers of these two species decreased in the late 1960s and were relatively low in the early 1970s (Table 8). DDE residues in heron livers decreased during the late 1960s and early 1970s. For total samples of sparrowhawk livers, there was little change in DDE content with time, but the trauma group of birds was more likely to be representative of that section of the population capable of laying eggs, and DDE in the livers of this group decreased during the late 1960s and early 1970s (Table 9; Cooke et al. 1979). The main difference between the changes in DDE content shown by eggs and livers was that from the early 1960s to the late 1960s: residues in eggs decreased whilst those in livers increased. This statement does not apply to the tissues and eggs of all species, however. DDE in the livers of kingfishers tended to

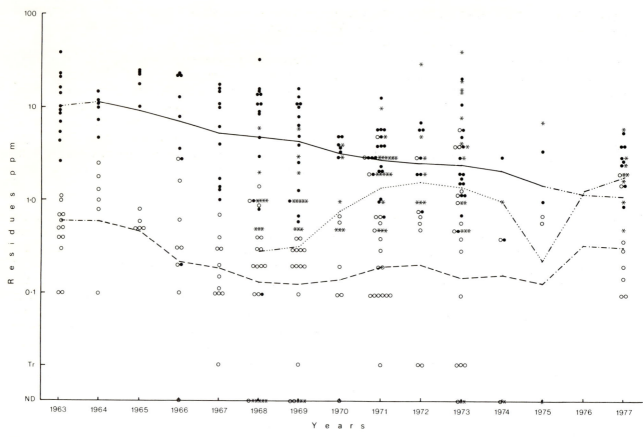

*Figure 35. Peregrine eggs: o, HEOD; ●, DDE; *, PCBs. Residues (one egg per clutch) year by year. 3-yearly trend in geometric means: — — —, HEOD (— · — · — ·, where 2-year values only available); ————, DDE (—··—··—); ...., PCBs (—···—····—).*

TABLE 33

Geometric mean residues in peregrine eggs.

		East & Central Scotland			Rest of Britain			Total samples	
	n	Geometric mean (ppm) (range of values within 1 standard error)		*n*	Geometric mean (ppm) (range of values within 1 standard error)		*n*	Geometric mean (ppm) (range of values within 1 standard error)	
HEOD									
1963–65	3	0.67	(0.54–0.82)	20	0.58	(0.47–0.71)	23	0.59	(0.49–0.71)
1966–71	26	0.06	(0.04–0.10)	50	0.20**	(0.16–0.27)	76	0.14***	(0.11–0.17)
1972–75	2	0.00		32	0.23	(0.15–0.36)	34	0.18	(0.11–0.28)
1977	0			12	0.34	(0.25–0.46)	12	0.34	(0.25–0.46)
ALL EGGS	31	0.06	(0.04–0.10)	114	0.27ª	(0.22–0.32)	145	0.20	(0.17–0.23)
DDE									
1963–65	3	6.84	(5.98–7.83)	20	12.2	(10.6–14.2)	23	11.3	(9.93–13.0)
1966–71	26	1.48***	(1.11–1.98)	50	5.62***	(4.79–6.60)	76	3.56***	(3.03–4.19)
1972–75	2	0.56	(0.40–0.80)	32	2.17***	(1.85–2.54)	34	2.01*	(1.71–2.35)
1977	0			12	2.42	(2.06–2.83)	12	2.42	(2.06–2.83)
ALL EGGS	21	1.62	(1.25–2.10)	114	4.51ª	(4.06–5.02)	145	3.62	(3.26–4.03)
PCBs									
1968–71	15	0.17	(0.09–0.33)	40	0.81	(0.62–1.06)	55	0.53	(0.40–0.70)
1972–75	2	0.10	(0.01–1.00)	32	1.04	(0.68–1.59)	34	0.90	(0.59–1.38)
1977	0			12	2.02	(1.86–2.19)	12	2.02	(1.86–2.19)
ALL EGGS	17	0.16	(0.09–0.29)	84	1.02ª	(0.82–1.25)	101	0.74	(0.60–0.92)

t-test: significantly different from previous period, *, $P<0.05$; **, $P<0.01$; ***, $P<0.001$.
significantly different from east and central Scotland, ª, $P<0.001$.

show a steady decline from 1964-1965 through into the 1970s (Table 19), while DDE in the eggs of shags taken from colonies on the Farne Islands (England) and Isle of May (Scotland) tended to show a peak in the late 1960s (Coulson *et al.* 1972).

Neither the sample of birds found dead, nor the sample of eggs collected from nests, need have been representative of the total population with respect to pollutant levels. With eggs, only birds with tissue residues below a certain level may have been capable of laying. As the incidence of sublethal and lethal effects due to pesticides declines, so the levels in tissues and eggs would be expected to decline in parallel. In the present situation, analysis of both carcases and eggs should give reasonable information on changes in levels of organochlorines in the species concerned

Analysis of herons' eggs indicated a local increase in PCB contamination in the Troy colony, although concentrations in eggs in other colonies, as in heron livers, did not rise at the same time. Throughout the 1970s, Newton and Bogan (1978, pers. comm.) monitored organochlorine levels in the eggs of sparrowhawks in a number of areas. Their results showed a general decline in HEOD concentration, but, for DDE and PCBs, some areas showed a decrease, some an increase, while in others concentrations remained unchanged. It would therefore be unwise to extrapolate the conclusions for a single area or colony to a wider region.

Seasonal variation was observed within each year in herons' eggs (Table 30). The only previous report of such variation in egg residues known to us is that of Robinson *et al.* (1967) on shags *(Phalacrocorax aristotelis)*. In this species the pattern of change varied from year to year, but within any one year the change in DDE content was similar to that for HEOD. With the heron eggs, there was no evidence for markedly different patterns of change in different years, but inevitably some of the sample sizes were small. Newton and Bogan (1978) found no seasonal change in the organochlorine content of sparrowhawk eggs laid at different dates over an eight-week period.

Where they occur, changes in the level of egg residues during the laying period are likely to be related to residue mobilisation and the increases in tissue residues noted previously. A bird whose fat reserves are metabolised would be likely to secrete larger amounts of organochlorines into its eggs. The egg is an efficient vehicle by which a female bird can rid itself of unwanted fat-soluble materials (eg see Bogan & Newton 1977). However, if the clutches collected from the heron nests in May were repeats, the evidence presented in Table 30 does not indicate that these were less contaminated than first clutches. In fact, few of the eggs were believed to be from re-laid clutches.

Calculations of geometric mean residues in eggs of the different species, collected in different regions, tended to confirm the conclusions of previous authors. In this report, only the sparrowhawk has been studied sufficiently intensively to determine geographical variations in both tissues and eggs. There was reasonable agreement between the two sets of data, with all residues tending to be higher in the East than in the North or West.

Eggs of the four species have all suffered considerable shell thinning in recent decades. Herons, sparrowhawks and peregrines continue to lay eggs with thin shells (Ratcliffe 1973; Mitchell 1976; Cooke *et al.* 1976; Newton & Bogan 1978). Golden eagles, on the other hand, have been only very lightly contaminated with DDE and HEOD, although breeding failure associated with organochlorine pollution has been observed in the west of Scotland where the highest residues occurred (Lockie & Ratcliffe 1964; Lockie *et al.* 1969; Ratcliffe 1970). In this species most of the blame for breeding failure was placed on HEOD and a "Decrease in residues of dieldrin in western Scottish golden eagles, subsequent to the banning of this chemical in sheep dips in 1966, was followed by partial recovery in eggshell thickness and marked improvement in breeding success" (Prestt & Ratcliffe 1972). The recovery in shell thickness for this species appears to have been complete by the late 1960s, although egg shells still tended to be weaker due to structural faults. That HEOD caused shell thinning in eggs of golden eagles is difficult to believe. Shell thinning appears to have occurred in this species in the early 1950s (Ratcliffe 1970) before dieldrin was widely used. In other species, DDE or other DDT-type compounds are considered to be responsible for shell thinning (Cooke 1973a, 1975). DDE levels decreased in eagle eggs concurrently with HEOD levels (Figure 33) and it seems reasonable to suggest that DDE, and not HEOD, caused the shell thinning (see also Newton 1979). HEOD may well have contributed to breeding failure because of its embryotoxic effects. Even quite small concentrations of DDE can cause appreciable shell thinning, and this explains why the other species continue to lay eggs with thin shells despite reductions in DDE concentrations.

Summary

1. More than 100 liver samples of each of four species — grey herons, sparrowhawks, kestrels and barn owls — were analysed for organochlorine residues during the period 1963-1977.

2. In a sample of kestrels, levels of organochlorines in the liver were positively related to levels in the brain.

3. Carcases were classified into groups according to the manner in which the birds died: trauma, poor-condition (including diseased) and remainder (miscellaneous causes of death, including suspected poisoning). Livers of birds in the remainder group tended to have higher residues than livers of birds that died through trauma.

4. Haemorrhage may be one symptom of poisoning by HEOD and perhaps by other organochlorines. Numbers of kestrels and sparrowhawks with haemorrhages and with different levels of HEOD in the liver were calculated for the remainder groups. For kestrels, the histogram was bimodal, with samples tending to contain either less than 5 ppm or more than 10 ppm HEOD. Those with the higher residues (67% of the samples) probably died from HEOD poisoning, while those with less than 5 ppm died from other causes. The histogram for sparrowhawk liver residues was different, the second (higher) peak was absent and only 16% of the samples contained more than 10 ppm HEOD. Further work is required on the causes of haemorrhages and on possible inter-species differences in sensitivity to HEOD.

5. For sparrowhawks in the trauma group, adults contained higher residues of DDE and PCBs in their livers than did juveniles. No other significant differences between age classes or sexes were noted among the trauma groups of sparrowhawk, heron or kestrel.

6. Adult sparrowhawks in the remainder group contained higher concentrations of all three residues than did juveniles. Females contained higher HEOD residues than males, and all nine birds with residues of 10 or more ppm HEOD were females (10 ppm is taken to be indicative of death by HEOD poisoning). Such high levels of HEOD were probably acquired from poisoned woodpigeons: only the larger female sparrowhawk is capable of killing woodpigeons.

7. Birds dying from trauma were examined to determine whether those of low body weight tended to have, on average, high HEOD residues. There was some tendency for this to occur in sparrowhawks and barn owls, but no such tendency was apparent in kestrels or herons.

8. Generally, birds in the poor-condition group tended to be of lower body weight than those in the respective trauma group, while birds in the remainder group were intermediate.

9. Birds (in the remainder group) with 10 or more ppm HEOD in the liver did not tend to have low body weights. Birds being removed from a population by HEOD poisoning were unlikely to be thin, sickly individuals, but were more probably otherwise fit and capable of breeding.

10. To examine seasonal, annual or regional trends, information for the trauma group and for total samples was treated separately. When mean residues were calculated for each species for each month, a consistent pattern emerged, with a peak almost invariably occurring during the second quarter of the year (April, May or June). This period also had the highest proportion of samples with residues of 10 ppm or more.

11. In kestrels, residues of organochlorines in both fat and liver were low in the autumn, but increased from about January. Fewer samples were available for sparrowhawks and barn owls, but these appeared to follow the same trend.

12. Body burden of organochlorines appeared to increase markedly during the early months of the year. Fat supplies were depleted in the spring, and liver residues rose appreciably. A similar seasonal peak occurred for all three of the main organochlorines. The observed seasonal changes in liver residues were likely to be due to physiological factors rather than to environmental ones.

13. Data for individual years were grouped into periods to test whether liver residue levels had changed significantly following the bans imposed on organochlorine usage. In kestrels and barn owls no significant differences in mean residues of HEOD were detected between the different periods until 1977, when means decreased. More detailed analysis revealed that HEOD residues in these two species tended to be low from 1975 and 1974 respectively. After a period of restricted use, HEOD was finally banned as a seed dressing at the end of 1975. Mean HEOD residues in heron livers decreased progressively from 1963-1965 to 1977. The main drop in HEOD content in the sparrowhawk occurred during the late 1960s; concentrations in livers tended to be high in 1967, but were extremely low from 1968 to 1971.

The bans imposed on various uses of dieldrin and other cyclodienes ultimately had the desired effect of lowering residues in avian tissues, but this reduction was not apparent in some species for several years. Dead kestrels and barn owls contained similar residues in the early 1970s to those found years earlier. However, the first (voluntary) ban on dieldrin and aldrin use occurred in 1961, and apparently produced an immediate reduction in residue levels just before our scheme started. Trends shown by pesticide residues in the Monks Wood programme were parallelled by findings of the MAFF PICL scheme on frequency of poisoning incidents over the years.

14. Herons, kestrels and barn owls generally showed increases in liver residues of DDE during the 1960s, but after the late 1960s these decreased, except for a peak in 1976 in kestrels. During this period, DDE residues in sparrowhawks did not change significantly. Information from the PICL scheme was again in agreement with these findings, since relatively large numbers of incidents were attributed to DDE in the late 1960s, and many incidents, apparently involving immigrant birds (including kestrels), were reported during 1976.

15. Liver residues of PCBs in herons, kestrels and barn owls have all shown a significant decline since the late 1960s, but only in kestrels did the decrease closely follow the restriction introduced by Monsanto in 1971. PCB residues in sparrowhawks did not change significantly.

16. Dieldrin and aldrin were probably used most in areas where cereals are at risk of attack from wheat bulb fly. Livers of herons, barn owls, and especially kestrels, had significantly higher HEOD residues inside the main wheat bulb fly areas than outside. Few sparrowhawks were received for analysis from these areas, but the same trend was apparent. This finding may indicate that birds found dead in these areas accumulated much of their HEOD from seed dressings (or other uses in arable agriculture).

17. It was in eastern England where avian tissues were most polluted with HEOD (excluding the extreme south-east). This region contains the main cereal-growing areas of Britain, where cyclodiene usage was especially high. On the other hand, DDE levels in livers were highest in south-east England. Fruit-growing becomes a progressively less important horticultural activity moving north. However, the uses of DDT on other crops must have contributed to the environmental contamination. Incidents involving birds flying from the European mainland and then dying from DDE poisoning in England are also more likely to occur in the south-east, this being the area closest to the continent. There were no clear regional trends in PCB residues, although liver residues in sparrowhawks, kestrels and barn owls tended to be comparatively low in Scotland.

18. Fifty-two and 63 liver samples of great crested grebes and kingfishers respectively were analysed between 1963 and 1977. Great crested grebes were relatively contaminated with DDE and PCBs, especially in south-east England. They contained very little HEOD in their livers, perhaps because the enclosed, isolated waters that they frequent remained comparatively free from HEOD. Kingfishers, however, were very contaminated with all three residues, although concentrations of HEOD and DDE tended to fall after the early 1960s. They showed a similar pattern of contamination to herons, which also feed on fish from flowing water. Geographical variations in contamination were, however, different between kingfishers and herons, and, for kingfishers, the origins of high residues of HEOD in the west and of DDE in the north-east remain uncertain.

19. In addition to the six species referred to above, fewer analyses were performed on the livers of ten other species. Carcases of golden eagles, rough-legged buzzards, peregrines and long-eared owls were collected from 1963 to 1977, while those of common buzzards, hen harriers, merlins, little owls, tawny owls and short-eared owls were restricted to 1963-1966. Because of the differences in the periods covered, residue levels in the two groups must be compared with caution.

20. Levels of HEOD, DDE or PCBs in the livers of the 16 species were examined in relation to the type of prey preferred. When species were arranged according to mean levels of HEOD, the order seemed independent of diet. At the top of the list were rough-legged buzzards, feeding on mammals and birds. Second were peregrines (birds), third long-eared owls (mammals and birds), and fourth kingfishers (fish). There was no reason to suppose that mammal-feeders would contain lower amounts than other species, since those feeding on rodents in agricultural situations were exposed to HEOD used as seed dressings. Barn owls and kestrels were sixth and seventh in the list. For DDE and PCBs, however, species that feed on birds or fish had higher liver residues than those that feed on mammals. Peregrines, herons, sparrowhawks, kingfishers and great crested grebes had relatively high residues of both DDE and PCBs. In contrast, golden eagles were only very lightly contaminated with all three organochlorines.

21. Populations of the three fish-eating species (heron, great crested grebe and kingfisher) have fared reasonably well in Britain, despite their high

pollutant residues. One possible explanation is that they escaped the lethal effect of HEOD, their intake of organochlorines generally being of a chronic rather than an acute nature. Also herons readily lay repeat clutches after breaking their first ones.

22. Only a small proportion of carcases contained sufficient organochlorine to suspect death from poisoning. HEOD seemed more important in this respect than DDE or PCBs. For example, 18% of all the kestrel livers analysed contained 10 ppm or more HEOD, a level taken to be indicative of death by HEOD poisoning. However, among kestrels from the east of England in the first six months of the year, this figure increased to 37%. It was in the east that problems due to organochlorines were most severe. Many more birds had liver residues of HEOD, DDE or PCBs high enough to have caused sublethal effects.

23. Some 50-150 livers were analysed for total mercury in sparrowhawks, kestrels and barn owls, but only 10 heron livers, covering the period 1968 to 1976. Herons contained significantly more mercury than the other species.

24. Mean mercury concentrations varied from month to month, and in sparrowhawks, kestrels and barn owls reached a peak in May and/or June, soon after moult began. However, sample sizes were small and further work is needed. In kestrels and barn owls, mercury levels increased again in November and December, perhaps due to ingestion of prey that had taken dressed grain.

25. In kestrels and barn owls mercury levels dropped significantly between 1970-72 and 1973-75 despite no restrictions having been imposed on the use of mercury in Britain.

26. Overall, mercury concentrations tended to be highest in East Anglia, the region where cereal growing is most intensive. Mean levels were consistently, although only slightly, higher in East Anglia than in the north and north-east. The west and south-east were intermediate.

27. At the Troy heronry, studied in particular detail, HEOD and DDE levels in eggs decreased from 1966 to 1970, but changed little thereafter. PCB levels tended to rise after 1970, a trend that was not apparent among the small numbers of eggs collected elsewhere.

28. Concentrations of HEOD, DDE and PCBs in heron eggs increased significantly during the laying season, March to May.

29. Few golden eagle eggs contained detectable amounts of PCBs. Residues of HEOD and DDE were low even in the early 1960s and declined during the second half of the decade. Eggs from western Scotland and the Hebrides contained significantly larger residues of HEOD and DDE than those from the central and eastern Highlands.

30. Mean DDE residues in sparrowhawk eggs declined during the late 1960s and early 1970s, whereas PCBs tended to increase during this period. HEOD residues were generally low from 1968 to 1970; they were highest in eggs collected in the east of Britain, while DDE and PCB residues were highest in the east and in the New Forest.

31. HEOD residues in peregrine eggs decreased in the mid-1960s. DDE residues decreased during the 1960s and early 1970s. Residues of PCBs were variable, tending to be highest in 1972 and 1977. Levels of HEOD, DDE and PCBs were lower in the east and central Highlands of Scotland than elsewhere in Britain.

32. Among the eggs of all four species, there was general agreement that residues of HEOD and DDE decreased appreciably during the latter part of the 1960s. Reductions in HEOD content may have been due to the restrictions imposed. There was no clear trend in PCB levels; in some species and regions there were indications of increases, but in others of decreases. Only in herons and sparrowhawks were changes in residue levels with time assessed in both livers and eggs. Generally, the trends were similar except for changes in DDE during the 1960s, which decreased in eggs but not in tissues. The discrepancy may have been due to the fact that neither the sample of birds found dead, nor the sample of eggs collected, was representative of the total living population with respect to pollutant levels.

33. Despite the fact that DDE levels in eggs have decreased, some herons, sparrowhawks and peregrines continue to lay eggs with thin shells. DDE levels will have to fall still further to rectify this problem. Golden eagles, which were relatively lightly contaminated with DDE even in the 1960s, now tend to lay eggs with shells of normal thickness.

Acknowledgements

More than 5300 specimens, mainly of predatory and aquatic birds and their eggs, were analysed during the 15-year period covered by this report.

Whilst it is obviously impossible to acknowledge individually the help of all the people concerned, special mention is made of the large number of Field and Regional Staff of the Nature Conservancy Council and the Royal Society for the Protection of Birds, who themselves contributed many specimens, and have often organised the collection of material in their regions when incidents occurred; the staff of the British Trust for Ornithology also supplied many carcases.

Thanks are also due to the many private individuals who have responded to published requests for specimens by troubling to pick up dead birds and post them to Monks Wood. Other observers have undertaken, often annually, the more difficult task of collecting material such as the failed eggs of peregrine and golden eagle. The help of all these contributors is greatly appreciated.

The RSPB journals 'Birds' and 'Bird Life' (Young Ornithologists' Club), those of the BTO, 'Bird Study' and 'BTO News', and the journals 'British Birds' and 'Scottish Birds' repeatedly published the requests for specimens without charge and often at short notice; the editors of all these publications are thanked for their co-operation.

Major Sir David Hawley Bt., Mr. J. L. Roughton J.P., and Messrs. J. L. Martin and Sons (Littleport) Ltd. granted us free access to study the heronries on their properties in Lincolnshire and Norfolk, and to collect eggs from these colonies, and Mr. A. E. Smith O.B.E., of the Lincolnshire Trust for Nature Conservation, kindly arranged for accommodation and laboratory facilities at the Gibraltar Point Field Station. A number of people, mainly staff at Monks Wood, helped with the periodic collection of eggs from the heronries.

The Forestry Commission readily gave permission to enter their forests in various parts of Britain to carry out surveys of breeding sparrowhawks, and many private landowners also allowed us unlimited access to their properties for the same purpose. Eggs were collected during these surveys.

The Laboratory of the Government Chemist carried out the many analyses required by the monitoring programme, and the efficient service afforded by Mr. D. C. Holmes and his staff is gratefully acknowledged. Dr. J. Robinson and the late Mr. A. Richardson of Shell Research Ltd. analysed some of the early heron eggs. Mr. M. C. French and his colleagues of ITE's Chemistry and Instrumentation Subdivision at Monks Wood also carried out analyses, and their help and advice over the years is appreciated.

This report documents the work of many people. Amongst those who have been responsible for the studies, the following are no longer at Monks Wood: Dr. D. J. Jefferies, Prof. N. W. Moore, the late Prof. R. K. Murton, Mr. J. L. F. Parslow, Mr. I. Prestt, Dr. D. A. Ratcliffe and Mr. C. H. Walker.

We are grateful to many colleagues in ITE for help and encouragment during the preparation of the manuscript. Dr. I. Newton has spent considerable time skilfully editing and condensing our original report to produce this final script. Mrs. S. Freestone deserves a special mention for some of the initial figure preparation and statistical calculation. We are also grateful to Dr. P. I. Stanley of the Ministry of Agriculture, Fisheries and Food for his help.

References

Ackefors, H. 1971. Mercury pollution in Sweden with special reference to conditions in the water habitat. *Proc. R. Soc. B.,* **177,** 365-387.

Advisory Committee on Poisonous Substances used In Agriculture and Food Storage. 1964. *Review of the persistent organochlorine pesticides.* London: HMSO.

Advisory Committee on Pesticides & other Toxic Chemicals. 1969. *Further Review of certain persistent organochlorine pesticides used in Great Britain.* London: HMSO.

Anon. 1978. Review of wildlife incidents. *Rep. Pest Infest. Control Lab., 1974-76,* 239-248.

Bailey, N.T.J. 1959. *Statistical methods in biology.* London: English Universities Press.

Bailey, S., Bunyan, P.J., Jennings, D.M., Norris, J.D., Stanley, P.I. & Williams, J.H. 1974. Hazards to wildlife from the use of DDT in orchards: II. A further study. *Agro-Ecosystems,* **1,** 323-338.

Bell, A.A. 1975. Dieldrin residues in the livers of kestrels and barn owls found dead in 1970-1973. *Annu. Rep. Inst. terr. Ecol. 1974,* 27-28.

Bell, A.A. & Murton, R.K. 1977. Dieldrin residues in carcases of kestrels and barn owls. *Annu. Rep. Inst. terr. Ecol. 1976,* 22-25.

Bell, A.A., Haas, M.B. & Murton, R.K. 1978. Mercury residues in carcases of kestrels, sparrowhawks and barn owls. *Annu. Rep. Inst. terr. Ecol. 1977,* 56-57.

Berg, A., Johnels, A., Sjöstrand, B. & Westermark, T. 1966. Mercury content in feathers of Swedish birds from the past 100 years. *Oikos,* **17,** 71-83.

Bogan, J.A. & Newton, I. 1977. Redistribution of DDE in sparrowhawks during starvation. *Bull. environ. Contam. & Toxicol.,* **18,** 317-321.

Bogan, J.A. & Newton, I. 1979. The effects of organochlorines on reproduction of British sparrowhawks *(Accipiter nisus).* In: *Animals as monitors of environmental pollutants,* edited by S. W. Nielsen, 269-279. Washington, D.C.: National Academy of Sciences.

Borg, K., Wanntorp, H., Erne, K. & Hanko, E. 1969. Alkyl mercury poisoning in terrestrial Swedish wildlife. *Viltrevy,* **6,** 301-379.

British Ornithologists' Union. 1971. *The status of birds in Britain and Ireland,* edited by D. W. Snow. Oxford: Blackwell Scientific Publications.

Brown, L. 1976. *British birds of prey.* London: Collins. (New Naturalist Series no.60)

Bull, K.R., Murton, R.K., Osborn, D., Ward, P. & Cheng, L. 1977. High levels of cadmium in Atlantic seabirds and sea-skaters. *Nature, Lond.,* **269,** 507-509.

Bunyan, P.J. & Stanley, P.I. 1973. *A review of wildlife incidents, attributable to the use of dieldrin as seed-dressing, investigated from 1963-1972 together with a detailed account of dieldrin incidents investigated in the spring of 1973.* Ministry of Agriculture, Fisheries and Food. Pest Infestation Laboratory. Wildlife Casualty Report no.2.

Bunyan, P.J., Stanley, P.I., Blunden, C.A., Wardall, G.L. &

Tarrant, K.A. 1975. The investigation of pesticide and wildlife incidents. *Rep. Pest Infest. Control Lab., 1971-73,* 211-222.

Clark, R.B. 1978. No refuge in the Zoo. *Mar. Pollut. Bull.,* **9,** 58-59.

Cook, J.W. 1964. — see Advisory Committee 1964.

Cooke, A.S. 1973a. Shell thinning in avian eggs by environmental pollutants. *Environ. Pollut.,* **4,** 85-152.

Cooke, A.S. 1973b. Response of *Rana temporaria* tadpoles to chronic dose of pp'-DDT. *Copeia,* **1973,** 647-652.

Cooke, A.S. 1975. Pesticides and eggshell formation. *Symp. zool. Soc. Lond.,* no. 35, 339-361.

Cooke, A.S., Bell, A.A. & Haas, M.B. 1979. *Birds of prey and pollutants; final report.* Natural Environment Research Council contract report to the Nature Conservancy Council. CST Report No. 256. Banbury: NCC.

Cooke, A.S., Bell, A.A. & Prestt, I. 1976. Egg shell characteristics and incidence of shell breakage for grey herons *Ardea cinerea* exposed to environmental pollutants. *Environ. Pollut.,* **11,** 59-84.

Coppock, J.T. 1964. *An agricultural atlas of England and Wales.* London: Faber & Faber.

Coulson, J.C., Deans, I.R., Potts, G.R., Robinson, J. & Crabtree, A.N. 1972. Changes in organochlorine contamination of the marine environment of eastern Britain monitored by shag eggs. *Nature, Lond.,* **236,** 454-455.

Cramp, S., Conder, P.J. & Ash, J.S. 1962. *Deaths of birds and mammals from toxic chemicals, January-June 1961.* The second report of the Joint Committee of the British Trust for Ornithology and the Royal Society for the Protection of Birds on Toxic Chemicals, in collaboration with the Game Research Association.

Davis, B.N.K. 1968. The soil macrofauna and organochlorine insecticide residues at twelve agricultural sites near Huntingdon. *Ann. appl. Biol.,* **61,** 29-45.

Department of the Environment. Central Unit on Environmental Pollution. 1976. Environmental mercury and man. *Pollut. Pap.* no.10.

Ecobichon, D.J. & Saschenbrecker, P.W. 1969. The redistribution of stored DDT in cockerels under the influence of food deprivation. *Toxicol. & appl. Pharmacol.,* **15,** 420-432.

Everett, M. 1977. *A natural history of owls.* London: Hamlyn.

Fuchs, P., de Vos, R.H. & Zwiers, J.H.L. 1971. Mercury in owls and birds of prey. *T.N.O. Nieuws,* **26,** 413-414.

Gough, H.C. 1957. Studies on wheat bulb fly *(Leptohylemyia coarctata* (Fall.)). IV. The distribution of damage in England and Wales in 1953. *Bull. ent. Res.,* **48,** 447-457.

Hatch, W.R. & Ott, W.L. 1968. Determination of sub-microgram quantities of mercury by atomic absorption spectrophotometry. *Analyt. Chem.,* **40,** 2085-2087.

HMSO. 1976. — see Department of the Environment 1976.

Hirons, G.J.M. 1976. *A population study of tawny owls, Strix aluco and its main prey species in woodland.* D. Phil. thesis: Oxford University.

Jefferies, D.J. 1967. The delay in ovulation produced by pp'-DDT and its possible significance in the field. *Ibis,* **109,** 266-272.

Jefferies, D.J. & Davis, B.N.K. 1968. Dynamics of dieldrin in soil, earthworms, and song thrushes. *J. Wildl. Mgmt,* **32,** 441-456.

Jefferies, D.J. & French, M.C. 1971. Hyper- and hypothyroidism in pigeons fed DDT: an explanation for the 'thin eggshell phenomenon'. *Environ. Pollut.,* **1,** 235-242.

Jefferies, D.J. & French, M.C. 1976. Mercury, cadmium, zinc, copper and organochlorine insecticide levels in small mammals trapped in a wheat field. *Environ. Pollut.,* **10,** 175-182.

Jefferies, D.J. & Parslow, J.L.F. 1976. Thyroid changes in PCB-dosed guillemots and their indication of one of the mechanisms of action of these materials. *Environ. Pollut.,* **10,** 293-311.

Jefferies, D.J. & Prestt, I. 1966. Post-mortems of peregrines and lanners with particular reference to organochlorine residues. *Br. Birds,* **59,** 49-64.

Jefferies, D.J., Stainsby, B. & French, M.C. 1973. The ecology of small mammals in arable fields drilled with winter wheat and the increase in their dieldrin and mercury residues. *J. Zool.,* **171,** 513-539.

Jones, D.M., Bennett, D. & Elgar, K.E. 1978. Deaths of owls traced to insecticide-treated timber. *Nature, Lond.,* **272,** 52.

Lockie, J.D. & Ratcliffe, D.A. 1964. Insecticides and Scottish golden eagles. *Br Birds,* **57,** 89-102.

Lockie, J.D., Ratcliffe D.A. & Balharry, R. 1969. Breeding success and organochlorine residues in golden eagles in west Scotland. *J. appl. Ecol.,* **6,** 381-389.

Łukowski, A.B. 1978. The content of organochlorine insecticides in the tissues of the great crested grebe *(Podiceps cristatus I)* and the coot *(Fulica atra* L.) from the Masurian lakes in different phenological periods. *Ekol. pol.,* **26,** 439-465.

Mead, C.J. 1973. Movements of British raptors. *Bird Study,* **20,** 259-286.

Mellanby, K. 1967. *Pesticides and pollution.* London: Collins. (New Naturalist Series no. 50).

Mitchell, J. 1976. *A report on the peregrine falcon in the Loch Lomond/Trossachs area of Scotland in 1976.* Mimeographed report.

Moore, N.W. 1965. Pesticides in birds — a review of the situation in Great Britain in 1965. *Bird Study,* **12,** 222-252.

Moore, N.W. & Walker, C.H. 1964. Organic chlorine insecticide residues in wild birds. *Nature, Lond.,* **201,** 1072-1073.

Moreton, B.D. & Kite, T.E 1975. DDT and birds in a Kentish orchard. *Bird Study,* **22,** 228-232.

Moriarty, F. 1975. *Pollutants and animals: a factual perspective.* London: Allen & Unwin.

Murton, R.K. 1971. *Man and birds.* London: Collins. (New Naturalist Series no. 51).

Newton, I. 1968. The temperatures, weights and body composition of moulting bullfinches. *Condor,* **70,** 323-332.

Newton, I. 1973. Egg breakage and breeding failure in British merlins. *Bird Study,* **20,** 241-244.

Newton, I. 1974. Changes attributed to pesticides in the nesting success of the sparrowhawk in Britain. *J. appl. Ecol.,* **11,** 95-102.

Newton, I. 1975. Movements and mortality of British sparrowhawks. *Bird Study,* **22,** 35-44.

Newton, I. 1979. *Population ecology of raptors.* Berkhamsted: Poyser.

Newton, I. & Blewitt, R.J.C. 1973. Studies of sparrowhawks. *Br. Birds,* **66,** 271-278.

Newton, I. & Bogan, J. 1974. Organochlorine residues, eggshell thinning and hatching success in British sparrowhawks. *Nature, Lond.,* **249,** 582-583.

Newton, I. & Bogan, J. 1978. The role of different organo-chlorine compounds in the breeding of British sparrowhawks. *J. appl. Ecol.,* **15,** 105-116.

Newton, I., Meek, E.R. & Little, B. 1978. Breeding ecology of the merlin in Northumberland. *Br. Birds,* **71,** 376-398.

Nicholson, E.M. 1929. Report on the "British Birds" census of heronries, 1928. *Br. Birds,* **22,** 270-323, 334-372.

Osborn, D. 1978. A naturally occurring cadmium and zinc binding protein from the liver and kidney of *Fulmarus glacialis,* a pelagic North Atlantic seabird. *Biochem. Pharmac.,* **27,** 822-824.

Osborn, D. 1979. Seasonal changes in the fat, protein, and metal content of the liver of the starling *(Sturnus vulgaris). Environ. Pollut.,* **19,** 154-155.

Osborn, D., Harris, M.P. & Nicholson, J.K. 1979. Comparative tissue distribution of mercury, cadmium and zinc in three species of pelagic seabirds. *Comp. Biochem, Physiol. C,* **64,** 61-67.

O'Shea, T.J. & Ludke, J.L. 1979. — see U.S. Department of the Interior 1979.

Parslow, J. 1973. *Breeding birds of Britain and Ireland.* Berkhamsted: Poyser.

Parslow, J.L.F. & Jefferies, D.J. 1975. Geographical variation in pollutants in guillemot eggs. *Annu. Rep. Inst. terr. Ecol., 1974,* 28-31.

Parslow, J.L.F. & Jefferies, D.J. 1977. Gannets and toxic chemicals. *Br. Birds,* **70,** 366-372.

Parslow, J.L.F., Jefferies, D.J. & Hanson, H.M. 1973. Gannet mortality incidents in 1972. *Mar. Pollut. Bull.,* **4,** 41-44.

Porter, R.D. & Wiemeyer, S.N. 1972. DDE at low dietary levels kills captive American kestrels. *Bull. environ. Contam. & Toxicol.,* **8,** 193-199.

Prestt, I. 1965. An enquiry into the recent breeding status of some of the smaller birds of prey and crows in Britain. *Br. Birds,* **12,** 196-221.

Prestt, I. 1970. Organochlorine pollution of rivers and the heron *(Ardea cinerea* L.). *Pap. Proc. Tech. Meet. int. Un. Conserv. Nat. nat. Resour., 11th, New Delhi, 1969,* **1,** 95-102. Morges, I.U.C.N.

Prestt, I. & Bell, A.A. 1966. An objective method of recording breeding distribution of common birds of prey in Britain. *Bird Study,* **13,** 277-283.

Prestt, I. & Jefferies, D.J. 1969. Winter numbers, breeding success, and organochlorine residues in the great crested grebe in Britain. *Bird Study*, **16,** 168-185.

Prestt, I. & Ratcliffe, D.A. 1972. Effects of organochlorine insecticides on European birdlife. *Int. orn. Congr.*, **15,** 486-513.

Prestt, I., Jefferies, D.J. & Macdonald, J.W. 1968. Post-mortem examinations of four rough-legged buzzards. *Br. Birds*, **61,** 457-465.

Prestt, I., Jefferies, D.J. & Moore, N.W. 1970. Polychlorinated biphenyls in wild birds in Britain and their avian toxicity. *Environ. Pollut.*, **1,** 3-26.

Ratcliffe, D.A. 1967. Decrease in eggshell weight in certain birds of prey. *Nature, Lond.*, **215,** 208-210.

Ratcliffe, D.A. 1970. Changes attributable to pesticides in egg breakage frequency and eggshell thickness in some British birds. *J. appl. Ecol.*, **7,** 67-115.

Ratcliffe, D.A. 1972. The peregrine population of Great Britain in 1971. *Bird Study*, **19,** 117-156.

Ratcliffe, D.A. 1973. Studies of the recent breeding success of the peregrine, *Falco peregrinus. J. Reprod. Fert., Suppl.*, **19,** 377-389.

Revzin, A.M. 1966. Effects of endrin on telencephalic function in the pigeon. *Toxicol. & appl. Pharmacol.*, **9,** 75-83.

Reynolds, C.M. 1974. The census of heronries, 1969-73. *Bird Study*, **21,** 129-134.

Robinson, J. 1967. Residues of organochlorine insecticides in dead birds in the United Kingdom. *Chemy Ind.*, November 25, 1967, 1974-1986.

Robinson, J. 1969. Organochlorine insecticides and bird populations in Britain. In: *Chemical fallout: current research on persistent pesticides*, edited by M.W. Miller and G.C. Berg, 113-173. Springfield, Illinois: Thomas.

Robinson, J. & Crabtree, A.N. 1969. The effect of dieldrin on homing pigeons (*Columbia livia* var.). *Meded. fakult. Landbouwwetenschappen Gent*, **34,** 413-427.

Robinson, J., Richardson, A., Crabtree, A.N., Coulson, J.C. & Potts, G.R. 1967. Organochlorine residues in marine organisms. *Nature, Lond.*, **214,** 1307-1311.

Sharrock, J.T.R. 1976. *The atlas of breeding birds in Britain and Ireland.* Berkhamsted: Poyser, for British Trust for Ornithology and Irish Wildbird Conservancy.

Sly, J.M.A. 1972. *Pesticide usage. Survey report 2: cereal seed dressing.* Pinner, Middlesex: Ministry of Agriculture, Fisheries and Food.

Snow, D.W. 1968. Movements and mortality of British kestrels (*Falco tinnunculus). Bird Study*, **15,** 65-83.

Srebocan, V., Gotal, J.P., Adamovic, V., Sokic, B. & Delak, M. 1971. Effect of technical grade DDT and p,p'-DDT on adrenocortical function in chicks. *Poult. Sci.* **50,** 1271-1278.

Stanley, P.I. & Elliott G.R. 1976. An assessment based on residues in owls of environmental contamination arising from the use of mercury compounds in British agriculture. *Agro-Ecosystems*, **2,** 223-234.

Stickel, W.H., Stickel, J.L. & Spann, J.W. 1969. Tissue residues of dieldrin in relation to mortality in birds and mammals. In: *Chemical fallout: current research on persistent pesticides*, edited by M.W. Miller and G.C. Berg, 174-200. Springfield, Illinois: Thomas.

U.S. Department of the Interior: Fish and Wildlife Service. 1979. *Monitoring fish and wildlife for environmental pollutants.* Fort Collins, Col.: U.S.D.I.

Vos, J.G., Strick, J.J.T.W.A., van Holsteyn, C.W.M. & Pennings, J.H. 1971. Polychlorinated biphenyls as inducers of hepatic porphyria in Japanese quail, with special reference to δ-aminolevulinic acid synthetase activity, fluorescence, and residues in the liver. *Toxicol. & appl. Pharmacol.*, **20,** 232-240.

Ward, P. 1978. Fat and protein reserves of starlings. *Annu. Rep. Inst. terr. Ecol., 1977,* 54-56.

Ward, P. 1979. *Heavy metals in waders overwintering in a polluted estuary: final report.* Natural Environment Research Council contract report to the Nature Conservancy Council. CST Report no. 253. Banbury: NCC.

Wilson, A. 1969. — see Advisory Committee 1969.

Yalden, D.W. & Warburton, A.B. 1979. The diet of the kestrel in the Lake District. *Bird Study*, **26,** 163-170.

Young, H. 1968. A consideration of insecticide effects on hypothetical avian populations. *Ecology*, **49,** 991-994.